GET

GET FINANCIALLY
SORTED BY 30

GET AHEAD . . .
GET FINANCIALLY
SORTED BY 30

The New Zealand way

Joan Baker
and
Annette Sampson

ALLEN&UNWIN

First published in 2004

Copyright © Joan Baker and Annette Sampson 2004

The information contained in this book is, to the best of the authors' and publisher's knowledge, true and correct. Every effort has been made to ensure its accuracy. Neither the author nor the publisher accepts any liability for any loss, injury or damage caused to any person acting as a result of information in this book, nor for any errors or omissions. Readers are advised to obtain professional investment advice before acting on the information contained in this book.

Allen & Unwin
83 Alexander Street
Crows Nest NSW 2065 Australia
Phone: (61 2) 8425 0100
Fax: (61 2) 9906 2218
E-mail: info@allenandunwin.com
Web: www.allenandunwin.com

National Library of Australia
Cataloguing-in-Publication entry:

Sampson, Annette.
  Get ahead : get financially sorted by 30 : the New Zealand
  way.

Includes index.
ISBN 1 74114 183 4.

1. Finance, Personal - New Zealand. 2. Saving and
investment - New Zealand. I. Baker, Joan, 1956- . II.
Title.

332.0240842

Cover Design: Zoe Sadokierski
Internal Design: Tabitha King
Illustrations: Gregory Roberts
Typesetter: Midland Typesetters, Maryborough, Victoria
Printer: Southwood Press, Sydney

CONTENTS

CHAPTER one
You *can* be financially set by 30

Just by picking up this book, you've taken a critical first step in the right financial direction. You're thinking about getting on top of your finances, and that's more than a lot of people are doing. The next step is to find the time to sit down, read and learn more about the smart—but simple— ways to get your money in order.

I'VE PICKED UP THE BOOK—BUT WHY SPEND MY VALUABLE SPARE TIME ON IT? PERSONAL FINANCE BOOKS TELL ME I SHOULD LIVE LIKE A MISER NOW SO THAT I CAN HAVE LOTS OF MONEY WHEN I'M ANCIENT. AND IT'S NOT AS THOUGH I HAVE LOTS OF SPARE MONEY, ANYWAY.

It's a real pain to be constantly told about the 'long term' when a lot of your financial worries and concerns are about here and now. That's why this book is targeted specifically at younger people—not people with mortgages and a tribe of kids, who are focused on issues like their kids' education, hair loss and retirement.

But it's really easy when you first start working to spend what you earn, borrow to buy things like cars and holidays, and end up at 25 or 30 deep in debt and wondering where all your money has gone.

If you're the sort of person who has good intentions, but seems to be constantly living from one pay to the next, it's time to get your finances in order. It could mean the difference between sinking into financial strife and really setting yourself up for the good life once you start earning more dollars.

Did you know that people under 30 make up one of the groups most likely to get into financial strife? Despite what you might think, it's not only big business-people who go broke. Ordinary Kiwis, who just don't know how to manage their finances, go broke too. For younger people, problem areas are credit cards, car accidents (where owners opt out of comprehensive or third-party insurance, have an accident and find themselves unable to pay the resulting bills), hire purchase and mobile phones. Along with perennials such as gambling and alcohol or drug abuse, of course.

But it's not all gloom and doom. There are also lots of other people in their twenties who may not be earning a lot, but manage their money so that they have a good time now and are setting themselves up to do even better in the future.

Whether it's your own home that you want, whether you want to start investing, or whether you simply want to have a bit of money left over out of each pay packet, the best time to start is before you're bogged down with financial commitments such as a mortgage and children.

Learning more about managing your money now can help you afford the things you want, as well as prepare you for the days when you do want to take on mortgages and other responsibilities.

IT SEEMS SO HARD TO GET STARTED—WAS IT THIS DIFFICULT FOR MUM AND DAD?

A lot of parents fall into the baby boomer generation who did have things pretty easy. The boomers were born after World War II (up to the early 1960s, in fact), and when they were your age, university was nearly free, they could pick and choose their jobs because unemployment was virtually unheard of, and they could buy houses at ridiculously low prices. A lot of people call them the lucky generation.

But there are advantages for you starting out now too. While it's not so easy to pick and choose jobs, younger people aren't locked into the rigid career structures their parents were. It's easier to throw in a job you don't enjoy to travel, study for something else, start up your own business or get a job doing something different, because the workforce is now more flexible and there are greater opportunities for things like contract and casual work. Nowadays, instead of thinking about a job for life, you develop a portfolio of skills that you can take from employer to employer.

Investing is also much easier than it was 20 or 30 years ago. We'll talk about investing in detail in Chapter 10, but let's just say now that there was a boom in the finance industry in the 1980s and 1990s and there are now so many investment products you can put your money into that it makes your eyes glaze over. Thanks to the Internet, it's easier than ever to get information on investments and the sharemarket, and you don't need a fortune to get started. The Internet has also made it easier to keep on top of your finances—so there's less excuse for being slack. If you can learn a lot about investment, you can take advantage of some of the great products that are now available.

And while house prices are high now, interest rates are relatively low and it's much easier than it used to be to borrow money. When your parents bought their first home, the odds are they had to grovel to their bank manager to get a loan. These days, a loan can be approved within a few hours, and if you don't want to go to them, chances are they'll come to you. Moreover, there are now a lot of different mortgage types available—things that can help you save a lot of money if you know how to take advantage of them. But the biggest advantage you have over your parents, and other older people, is time. You've got all the time in the world to make mistakes and learn from them, and you've also got time to take advantage of compound interest, which helps your money grow.

COMPOUND INTEREST? YUCK! SOUNDS LIKE SOMETHING THEY TEACH YOU IN ECONOMICS.

Compound interest is one of the most basic—and effective—ways of growing money. And it's dead simple: instead of just earning interest on your money each year, you reinvest it and earn interest on your interest. If you do this for long enough, you'll have piles of cash that you didn't have to save or earn yourself, and which earns more money for you each year. It's the closest thing we've got to money for nothing.

How does it work?

Let's take a very simple example. Let's say you and your dad both find $1000 to invest. You're both prepared to leave the money untouched until you're 50 and add the interest you earn to your investment, instead of spending it. Let's say you're 25 now, Dad is 45, and you're both earning an interest rate of 5 per cent.

Not taking tax into account, your dad will have $1276 when he turns 50. But you, with all that extra time, will have $3386 by the time you're 50. You'll have tripled your money and, in your 26th year, you will earn around $170 in interest, even though you've only invested $1000 at a measly 5 per cent.

And if you're smart about where you put your money, compound interest gets even better. If you and Dad were earning 10 per cent interest instead of 5 per cent, you'd have $10 835 by the time you're 50, compared to Dad's $1610.

This graph shows how compound interest really accelerates the longer you have to invest. See how it takes off like a rocket after the first five or so years?

You've probably seen all those ads that show similar benefits if you start to invest early. It's nothing more than simple compound interest. And the younger you are when you start, the easier making money becomes.

So what are you waiting for?

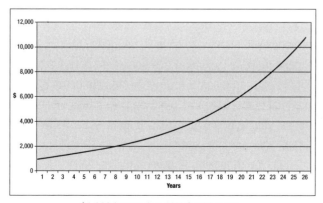

$1,000 invested at 10% for 25 years

CHAPTER two
Earning it—pay cheques and balances

To make money you do have to have some money to start with. But your most valuable move is looking at this book right now. It's about you and your ability to earn an income. A 20-year-old who earns $30 000 a year will earn a total of more than $1.3 million during their working life. And if you increase your earning potential, it gets even better. If you earn $40 000 p.a., your earning potential is close to $2 million, and if you hit the big league, you're looking at several million dollars. Now is the time to be looking to increase your earning potential—whether it's getting ahead in your current job or preparing yourself for a better one.

I'M CONFUSED ABOUT MY WORK ENTITLEMENTS—HOW DO I FIND OUT WHAT I SHOULD BE GETTING?

All employees in New Zealand are covered by some form of employment agreement. Some will be covered by a collective agreement that has been negotiated by a union, others will have an individual agreement. The law now requires these agreements to be in writing. The agreement must include a job description, hours of work and the wages or salary paid. There are minimum legal requirements for holidays and other leave and an employer cannot offer you less.

If you have any doubt about the agreement covering your job you should ask your employer or union organiser for a copy. Agreements are negotiable: the individual or the union can negotiate the details of the contract. Both parties must negotiate 'in good faith'.

Your employer cannot change your employment contract without your agreement. If you do not sign the new contract offered you will continue to be employed under the old agreement.

The Employment Relations Service has a very good Website at www.ers.dol.govt.nz or they can be called on 0800 800863.

Your local Citizens Advice Bureau has many useful pamphlets related to work and your entitlements and there is usually someone available to point you in the right direction.

HOW MUCH SHOULD I BE PAID?

You should try to get paid as highly as possible for all the obvious reasons! However, it can take some training, skills and experience before you get paid a great deal. There are legal minimums:

- 16–17 year olds have to be paid a minimum of $6.80 per hour (that equates to $54.40 for an 8-hour day , and $272.00 for a 40-hour week)
- Adults (18 and over) have to be paid a minimum of $8.50 an hour (that equates to $68.00 for an 8-hour day and $340.00 for a 40-hour week)

Neither you nor your employer can contract out of these minimums, i.e., you cannot agree to pay or be paid less. By law, your employer is required to deduct tax from your pay under the PAYE (Pay As You Earn) system. If you have a student loan the IRD will require that repayments are deducted from your wages as soon as your earnings reach a threshold of $15 964.00. If you are liable for child support the IRD may require your employer to deduct that as well. Nothing else should be deducted from your pay unless you have agreed in writing, for example, you might agree for your employer to deduct superannuation payments.

If you have problems or concerns about your pay or other conditions and cannot get these resolved by your supervisor (or for some reason feel you cannot approach that person directly) there are several organisations that may be able to help:

The Human Rights Commission can be called on 0800 496877 or accessed at www.hrc.govt.nz. The Employment Relations Service have a very helpful Website (see above). People covered by a union-negotiated award can contact the Council of Trade Unions on 04 385 1334 or log on to their site at www.union.org.nz. Inland Revenue also have an excellent site (www.ird.govt.nz) where you can get information about deductions and about paying off your student loan.

HOW CAN I INCREASE MY PAY?

Employers pay more for qualifications, skills and experience. It is worth your time, effort and even some financial investment to improve your qualifications and build your skills. A relatively small increase in wages or salary now will compound over the years. Some employers have agreements in place that offer pay rises for specific skills (skills-based pay). Qualifications are not the only factor involved in setting pay rates, but, overall, the international evidence suggests that additional years at school and qualifications and training usually mean that people earn more money each year over their working life.

People who want to become better off usually put a great deal of effort into saving and investing (more about that later). However, sometimes the easiest way to grow your wealth is to raise your income. Many people are far more focused on trying to spend less rather than trying to earn more! The payoff for younger people is greatest—if you can make yourself more valuable now you can reap the benefits of that extra income over the next 40–50 years.

Many employers are very willing to subsidise your ongoing education—some will agree to pay the full fees for courses you take; others may share the cost. Some will even give you some time off for classes. If you are lucky enough to have such a good employer you should not hesitate to take advantage of these opportunities: someone else is helping you make yourself more valuable and that value will be yours for the rest of your life.

There is a huge range of development opportunities available, including classes at your local high school (community education), courses offered through polytechnics and private training establishments, and a huge offering of distance education programmes from universities, Wananga, The Open

Polytechnic, etc. The range is very wide and there is something to suit almost everyone. While you (or your employer) will probably have to make some investment, education in New Zealand is still very cost effective and heavily subsidised by Government.

The National Qualifications Framework allows you to accumulate credit for the learning that you do and, over time, acquire nationally recognised Certificates, Diplomas and even Degrees. This means that even if you left school with few credits you can start over at whatever level you need and continue from there.

The New Zealand Qualifications Authority (NZQA) has a very good Website (www.nzqa.govt.nz) that will let you explore some of the options. Many of the education providers also have good sites—check out The Open Polytechnic at www.openpolytechnic.ac.nz and any polytechnic or private training providers near you. If you wish to work towards recognised qualifications you need to make sure that both the institution and the course have been approved by NZQA.

I'M THINKING OF CHANGING JOBS—HOW DO I GET A BETTER DEAL FROM MY NEW BOSS?

There's a real thrill in finding a new job—especially if you were feeling bored or unappreciated in your old one. But this is the time when you need to keep a clear head.

Make sure you update your CV (or curriculum vitae—Latin for 'course of life'—should detail your education, qualifications, what you have achieved to date, your previous employment, projects undertaken, etc.) and present it as well as you can. Your CV is like a sales folder—it is selling you! Make it as impressive as you can—if you have letters of thanks from managers or customers you should include them. It's definitely worth including photographs of events or projects you have participated in, or folios of work that showcase your skills.

Before you accept a new job, think about what you'll bring to the position and what you want from it. If aspects of the job bother you, or some of the conditions are unacceptable, now is the time to say so. You lose all your bargaining power once you're on the payroll. Most employers won't be impressed if you're all smiles during the interview, but try to change the rules as soon as you're in the job.

When negotiating salary and conditions, emphasise what you think you'll be able to achieve in the job. You'll have a much better chance of convincing your new boss to pay you more if you can show how they will benefit from hiring you. Remuneration consultants say qualifications have less clout than they used to have—these days more and more people have got them. But good track records are highly sought after, so emphasise what you have achieved in the past, how it benefited previous employers, and what value you'll be bringing to the employer's business. Think about it from the employer's point of view—why should they hire you? Why should they pay you more? What evidence are you offering them that you are worth more? Employers generally focus on three key areas:

1 **Can you do the job?** In other words have you got the qualifications or skills to carry out the role that they are seeking to fill. You will want to present evidence of your education or training or the skills and competencies that you have acquired. Without evidence that you are likely to be able to do the job, you do not get past this point in the process.
2 **Will you do the job?** The prospective employer will look for evidence of previous performance. Can you show that you have achieved good results in other jobs or on other

occasions? What evidence can you produce that you are responsible, will get things done, will follow through and are reliable in carrying out your tasks? Even if you have very little work experience you will want to show as much performance as you can in sport, charitable work, or other extra-curricular activities.

3 **Will you fit in**? Smart employers are usually seeking a person with a good attitude who has developed attractive interpersonal skills. Can you show that you are a pleasant person to work with and that you have a track record of getting on well with others?

Don't undersell yourself; but don't make the mistake of pitching too high against the rest of the market either. In some cases, it may be better to settle for a little less than you wanted at first, but to get a written agreement that, if you meet certain goals, your pay will be increased after six or 12 months.

MONEY ALERT

According to Wagenet (a useful Australian site at www.wagenet.gov.au) here are some common traps to watch out for when accepting a new job:

- **Trial periods on the job without payment**. A good employer will tell you how long the trial will last and pay you a proper wage during the trial period

- **Employers who don't give you job offers in writing**. This is unprofessional on their part and downright dangerous for you. You should get a formal letter of appointment and it should cover your terms of employment as well as any extra agreements you came to—like that upcoming pay review. The law requires a written agreement.

- **Employers who don't pay you on time**.

- **Jobs which pay only by commission**. Apart from the fact that you're taking all the risks, there's also a risk you may be classed as self-employed rather than as an employee. This means that you will not have the protection that employees have under the law.

ARE THERE ANY ADVANTAGES TO CASUAL OR PART-TIME WORK?

Flexibility's an obvious advantage for casual and part-time workers. You're better able to choose your work hours and you may be able to juggle several jobs at a time. It's a matter of what you're most comfortable with.

Both part-time and casual workers will also be covered by a contract that will set out their rates of pay and conditions. Generally, part-time employees work a regular number of hours each week and receive an hourly rate equal to that of a full-time worker doing the same job. Sometimes you'll get a bit more. Part-time employees generally receive all, or most of, the benefits of full-time employees but on a 'pro rata' basis. An example of a part-time employee might be someone who works three days each week instead of five.

Casual workers work on an hourly or daily basis. Unlike part-time employees, their hours can change from week to week depending on when they're needed. Casual workers get an extra loading on top of the normal rate to compensate for the fact that they don't receive benefits such as sick leave and paid holidays. In some industries, casuals get paid a hefty loading compared with ordinary employees. This can make casual work a great way to earn some extra money quickly. But ordinary employees are guaranteed a set number of hours each week, which casuals are not. Many casuals work through employment agencies, which aim to provide them with regular work—though the agency takes a portion of the employer's payments for itself.

So it's a question of which best suits you.

One of the hidden snags in part-time or casual work is that you do not usually get much training or development. Employers are often reluctant to invest in you if they feel you are only partly committed to them or only in their business occasionally.

This may not impact on your take-home pay in the short term but may mean you are relatively poorly paid over the years. It's very bad for your long-term work career as you may miss out on developing the skill set that you need to progress. In addition, part-time and casual workers have difficulty building up a good track record of employment (CV) that will get them well-paid secure work in the future.

You should probably consider part-time or casual work for special situations only: when you are waiting for full-time work; when you are still studying; or when you have to care for small children, etc.

I WANT MORE MONEY—HOW DO I NEGOTIATE A PAY RISE?

Three words: preparation, preparation, preparation. Telling an employer 'I'm worth more', 'I can't live on what you're paying me', or 'I might as well stay at home and do nothing for what I'm paid' is a fast way to totally ruin any chance of getting more money.

Your employer will have a stream of arguments to counter your push for a pay rise, so you need to be ready to put your case convincingly. The best advice is to be professional, rather than making a personal appeal. You have to present your case in commercial terms and emphasise the value you're bringing to the business. In short, you've got to be able to show exactly why you're worth more.

And if at first you don't succeed, keep trying. There's truth in the saying that it's the squeaky wheel that gets fixed.

If you're offered a job elsewhere, this can also be a good bargaining tool—even if you don't want to take the other job. It's not fair, but the fact is that most employers value you more if they think someone else is interested in you. You don't have to march in and say, 'X has offered me more money than you and I'm leaving unless you match it'. In fact, that's asking for trouble—unless you genuinely want the other job.

Instead, have a quiet chat with your boss. Tell them you've been approached by someone else who offered you more money but you would prefer to stay where you are. Tell your boss the offer made you think about your prospects within their company and your value to it. Use the interview as an opportunity to get a feel for whether you're genuinely better off staying where you are, or whether you should take the other job.

SMART TIP

It can also pay to think laterally in terms of how you are paid.

Performance-linked pay is on the rise and can often break the stalemate where you want more money and your employer is not prepared to exceed a certain limit. The most common form of performance pay is a bonus, which is paid only if you meet certain agreed targets.

Of course your job needs to be measurable in some way for you to negotiate a bonus. And the targets and terms of payment will need to be clearly spelt out in your employment contract. But it's worth thinking about what you're bringing to a company, and whether your performance can be rewarded by a bonus system. Many larger companies now pay team bonuses or have profit sharing arrangements so that all employees benefit from improved performance.

The most effective way to get paid more is to make yourself more valuable. We have already discussed acquiring more education and further skills. If you are lucky your employer may provide lots of training and development at work and at the employer's expense. Avail yourself of every opportunity. If you are less fortunate and little is provided at your workplace you should decide to take responsibility for your own upskilling and further education—after all, you will be the main beneficiary and almost certainly will be more employable and earn better money for the rest of your working life.

Not only are better educated and skilled employees worth more to their employer but the fact that you are keen to learn and have taken the initiative to develop your skills will impress most employers. You will get noticed; your employer will take more interest in you; they will be keen to keep you; and you will have better negotiating power. These are very good returns for a relatively small investment on your part.

After all, you are your own most valuable asset: invest in yourself. The payoff is usually very good—and far less risky than some other investments we will discuss in later chapters.

CAN I ASK MY EMPLOYER TO HELP ME UPGRADE MY SKILLS?

Many employers have training policies and are only too willing to help employees gain more skills. If the skills you want will benefit you in your job, or help you advance in the company, your employer may even be prepared to help fund external studies—or give you study leave to undertake the course. It never hurts to ask anyway—even if your employer will not help it sends a signal that you are interested in your own future and prepared to take the initiative to develop yourself.

WHAT'S SALARY PACKAGING? CAN IT HELP ME INCREASE MY INCOME?

Another way to get more bang for your work buck is to look at salary packaging. This means that you trade off part of your pay for extra fringe benefits. Salary packaging has become much less effective since the introduction of Fringe Benefits Tax (FBT), which taxes your employer on most benefits, but there are still some benefits that can be provided at less cost to your employer than if you had paid for them yourself out of your after-tax salary.

Superannuation is one, but we'll discuss that in more detail later in this chapter. Does your employer offer an employee share scheme? These schemes allow you to buy shares in the company you work for with pre-tax dollars, or to defer the tax payable. One common scheme allows you to sacrifice around $1000 of your before-tax salary each year to buy shares in the company, and the shares are tax free. Another scheme allows you to sacrifice larger amounts with no income tax payable until you sell the shares. Other benefits that can be used to spice up your pay package include laptop computers, mobile phones, employer-provided gyms, airline club memberships, briefcases, electronic diaries, taxis to and from work, financial planning, home offices, professional subscriptions and income protection insurance.

Talk to your employer about the benefits they can offer and the after-tax effect on your pay package.

WHAT ABOUT A COMPANY CAR?

Cars are probably the most common benefit. Some jobs, for example, many sales roles, need a car and businesses commonly provide cars for these roles. You may be able to use the car in the evenings, weekends, or on your private holidays. You may have to sacrifice some salary for the use of a company car. The business will have to pay Fringe Benefit Tax (FBT) if you are provided with a car for private use. Depending on your position and the quality of car provided, you may have to sacrifice a little or a lot of your salary. You should consider the offer of a company car in the light of your personal circumstances: do you already have a car? Does it seem like a good deal? Convenience is often the deciding factor—company cars are usually maintained, registered and warranted by the company which can be especially useful if you are very busy.

WHAT'S SUPER?

Super (superannuation) is money put aside in a special fund for your retirement. You often can't take the money out until you retire. Sometimes your employer will offer you membership in a super scheme that it subsidises. If your workplace has such a scheme you should consider it carefully—they are usually a good deal because of the money contributed by your employer. You can elect to join a super scheme yourself and your employer will usually agree to have deductions made from your salary directly into the super scheme. This is all your money of course—but it is a form of disciplined saving and you don't have the bother or the temptation of handling the money yourself. Superannuation in New Zealand is 'tax neutral', that is, it is no better or worse than any other form of saving for your retirement. You do not get any tax incentives in NZ for saving for your retirement so you need to think carefully about how you accumulate money for later years. In many other countries, including Australia, superannuation is both compulsory (deducted from salary at source) and taxed concessionally. You are on your own in NZ!

HOW DO SEVERANCE PAYMENTS WORK?

A so-called 'severance payment' can usually be broken down into three components, which are:

- Unused annual leave. This is taxed as ordinary income.
- Any accrued long-service leave. This is also taxed as ordinary income.
- A redundancy payment. Redundancy payments are becoming less and less common. There is no requirement for employers to pay redundancy unless it is specifically required by your employment contract. Nevertheless some employers do make redundancy payments even when not required to do so. These are also taxed.

If you're looking at serious money, you should talk to a financial planner about the best thing to do with your severance payment.

IS SETTING UP MY OWN BUSINESS WORTH IT?

If you want to know whether it's worth setting up your own business, have a look at the annual *National Business Review* list of New Zealand's richest people. You will see names like Graeme Hart, Eric Watson and Doug Myers. They're not doctors or accountants; the vast majority of them are people with their own businesses. Okay, so some people had family money to start with. It helps, but it isn't essential. Success stories also include people who started with nothing and are now worth squillions. Most of these people have become rich by owning a business.

But before you get too carried away with the idea of making your fortune, it's a good idea to have a hard think about whether running a business is what you want from life. Not all of us are suited to running a business; for those who don't get a thrill from the chase, it can be a hard slog. Most people with businesses work long hours and success does not happen overnight. It is often years before there is a good payoff.

Fans of the TV series 'SeaChange' might recall Angus, the mad surfer, who worked as a clerk at the local court. In one episode, Angus was approached to set up a business to manufacture the surfboard he had designed. A large company was interested in buying into Angus' company, but at one point in the negotiations Angus said something like, 'But when will I have time to go surfing?'

Just because you like doing something doesn't mean you'll enjoy running a business in that area. In many cases, it's a perfect way to ruin a good hobby.

SMART TIP

If you're thinking about going into business, ask yourself these questions:

- Do I really want to run a business? Will I enjoy the process of selling my product or services? Who will take care of the finances?

- What qualities or skills do I have to make the business work? Can I sell? How will I be dealing with customers? Do I have a good idea? Do I have the discipline to turn that idea into a successful business?

- Am I prepared to work long hours on a tiny wage to get the business up and running? How much of a time and financial commitment am I prepared to make?

- Am I a risk taker? Can I handle not having a regular income to rely on? How do I feel about the possiblity that in five years I could be a millionaire, dead broke or exactly where I am now?

WHERE DO I START IF I HAVE A GOOD IDEA FOR A BUSINESS?

The first step is to do a business plan. People talk about business plans as though they're hopelessly complicated and you need an MBA to do them. That's nonsense. All you need to do is to write down the basics of the business:

- Who you'll be selling to: How big is your target market? How do you reach them? Who are your competitors? And what advantage do you have over the competition?
- Your costs: How much will it cost to buy in the products or services you need? Will you need to rent business premises? Do you need to borrow money? How much?
- Your income: What can you charge for your product or service? How much do you need to sell to cover your costs? Is this achievable? How long will it take?

Rob Bastion (a former CE of the Council of Small Business Associations of Australia) says you should always allow a hefty margin for error. Overestimate your costs and underestimate your income and, if it still looks like a viable proposition, then consider the next step.

SMART TIP

Bizinfo is your starting point for information and contacts. Bizinfo has offices in most major centres and can be accessed online at www.bizinfo.co.nz or by phone on 0800 424946. They also produce some very useful brochures and run good programmes, many of which are free.

Business groups such as the Chamber of Commerce (www.chamber.co.nz) can also put you on to people who can help. A good accountant can help you refine your numbers, and you'll probably need to invest in a software package, such as Quicken or MYOB, to track your finances.

CHAPTER three
So what's the problem?

Okay, so there's money coming in, even if it's not a fortune. Now you have to make a firm decision to manage that money effectively—and complaining that you don't have enough money isn't going to get you there. What do you need to know to get started?

I DON'T HAVE ENOUGH MONEY TO PAY MY EXPENSES—HOW CAN I START UNTIL I'M EARNING MORE MONEY?

It's Murphy's law of finance: we always earn less than we need. A few years back, the *New Zealand Herald* received a letter to the financial adviser. It was from a young IT worker who was complaining that he couldn't pay his bills and was running up debts—even though he earned $150 000. Most of us find that pretty ludicrous, but it emphasises the point that our spending tends to expand as our income rises.

The popular TV series, 'The Money Doctors', revealed that many people who earned quite reasonable amounts of money had great difficulty living within their means and managing their personal finances.

Living within your means sounds boring, and it can be painful at first, but it works. The best way around the problem is to set yourself some financial goals. The goals don't have to be virtuous. It might be that you'd really love to be able to take a year off work to travel or to buy a new car without going into hock for it. Or perhaps you want to buy your own home—your goal could be to save the deposit.

Have some fun with your goals. Draw up a list of what you'd really like, set some priorities, and put a realistic time-frame on it. You'll be surprised how much easier it is to save once you have a good reason to do so.

OK, SO I'VE SET MY GOALS—HOW DO I LIVE WITHIN MY MEANS?

Here's where we mention the B-word. You start off by doing a budget. People tend to cringe when the B-word is mentioned, but it's really nothing more than a list of what you earn and where it's spent. You can do it on a monthly or an annual basis. A lot of people prefer monthly because it is easier to work out the expenses on a monthly basis. However, a lot of people like to base the time periods on their budget around when they get paid, which could see you doing it on a weekly or fortnightly basis. But don't forget less frequent expenses such as phone and electricity bills, car registration, insurance, gym memberships, and so on. These can be divided up on a monthly basis.

You can do a budget manually (i.e., on a piece of paper) or electronically on your computer. If you are going to do it on a computer, you should go to www.sorted.org.nz. This has a lot of financial information including templates to set up your budget. You can save what you do and then go back to it when you want. The site will prompt you to make sure that you include all your likely expenditure items.

To do a budget manually, sit down with a piece of paper and divide it in half vertically. On one side list your income.

As well as your salary, your income should include any interest you receive, dividends from shares, regular overtime, investment income, and so on.

Then, on the other side of the paper, list your expenses.

Expenses take more time and generally fall into three categories—fixed, essential and discretionary.

Fixed expenses are money you *have* to spend. They include rent (or mortgage repayments), repayments on other loans or leases, insurance premiums, and so on. Essential expenses are also money you have to spend, but these expenses can vary. They include food, clothing, electricity, water, phone and gas bills, medical costs and transport. Discretionary expenses are expenses over which you have complete control. Most of your discretionary expenses will be entertainment—money spent on sport or hobbies, movies, eating out or takeaway meals, holidays, mobile phones and the Internet, gifts, Friday night drinks, shopping sprees . . . you get the picture.

Try to be realistic. Budgets work on the 'garbage in, garbage out' or GIGO principle: they're only as good as the information you put into them. Your budget is a tool to help you manage your money better, not a report card.

If you are genuinely at a loss as to what you spend, try keeping careful track of your expenses for a month and then doing the budget. But don't forget to allow for those annual expenses.

The difference between your income and expenses is the money you have available for saving. If it is negative, you have a problem. You're spending more than you earn. If it is positive, the question is whether it is enough to meet your financial goals.

SMART TIP

If you don't want to do the sums yourself, there are some great online budget tools that tote up the figures for you. There's a good one on *www.sorted.org.nz* you can try for starters. Or use the one I've provided on the next page.

I'M PRETTY SURE I KNOW HOW I SPEND MY MONEY—WHY DO I NEED TO WRITE IT DOWN?

If you genuinely know where your money goes, you're one of a select few. Most of us—the authors included—get a few nasty shocks when we take the trouble to write down our expenses, which is probably why we hate doing so.

Even if you've got a pretty good idea of what you spend, having your expenses written down allows you to look at them more objectively. It's easier to see where you can cut your spending and by how much. Whenever we do a budget,

D	INCOME	$
	Your salary (after tax)	. . . .
I	Dividends	. . . .
	Interest	. . . .
	Managed fund distributions	. . . .
	Other	. . . .
Y	TOTAL INCOME	. . . .
	FIXED EXPENSES	
	Rent/mortgage repayments	. . . .
	Contents/home insurance	. . . .
B	Car insurance	. . . .
	Car registration	. . . .
	Student loan	. . . .
U	Loan repayments	. . . .
	....	. . . .
	....	. . . .
D	....	. . . .
	FIXED EXPENSES TOTAL	. . . .
G	ESSENTIAL EXPENSES	
	Food	. . . .
E	Clothing	. . . .
	Phone	. . . .
	Mobile phone	. . . .
T	Electricity	. . . .
	Home maintenance	. . . .
	Car running costs	. . . .
	Taxis/public transport	. . . .
P	....	. . . .
	....	. . . .
	....	. . . .
	ESSENTIAL EXPENSES TOTAL	. . . .
L		
	DISCRETIONARY EXPENSES	
A	Sport/hobbies	. . . .
	Entertainment—movies, etc	. . . .
	Eating out/takeaways	. . . .
N	Internet	. . . .
	Holidays	. . . .
	Partying	. . . .
N	Gifts	. . . .
	Household goods/furnishings	. . . .
	....	. . . .
E	....	. . . .
	....	. . . .
	DISCRETIONARY EXPENSES TOTAL	. . . .
R	TOTAL EXPENSES	. . . .
	SURPLUS/SHORTFALL	. . . .

we're always surprised at how much the little things add up. By being conscious of how catching a taxi to work pushes up your transport bill, for example, you're more inclined to rethink that urge to jump into a cab. For other people we know, it's takeaway food, coffee, or cigarettes, that eat up the dollars. Doing a budget makes you more conscious of where your spending weaknesses are.

If you're really keen to make budget savings, you can also keep your written budget and check your actual expenditure against it from time to time to see how your economising efforts are faring. Carry a notebook with you and jot down every expenditure that you make (even the $1 you paid for a newspaper). After a few weeks this will become a painless habit that will help you identify any overspending and call a halt before it becomes a problem.

Alternatively, it may help you find opportunities to save more.

I'VE INHERITED NONE OF MY MOTHER'S SAVING HABITS—HOW CAN I CHANGE THIS?

Doing a budget and knowing where your money goes is a great start. If you know you have a weakness for spending in certain areas, you can also take steps to avoid temptation. A friend's problem used to be going to the ATM when she was having a night out and had spent her allocated drinking money. She was having too much fun to go home and taking more money out of the ATM was so easy she didn't even stop to think about the impact on her budget.

The cure? She went cold turkey. She left her ATM card at home when she knew she was going to have a night out. Sure, she could still borrow money or find a way to overspend, but it was harder. And as time passed, she found her spending patterns changed so that she could manage on the cash that she had allocated herself.

If impulse spending on credit cards is your weakness, why not try leaving the cards at home? If you see something you want, you can always come back and buy it tomorrow. But you've given yourself time to think about whether it's something you really want, or just something that grabbed you at the time.

Similarly, if your wardrobe is full of clothes that you never wear, try making a resolution not to buy anything without getting a friend's opinion on whether it suits you. Again, you're giving yourself a chance to avoid wasteful spending and ensuring that if you do spend, your money is buying something you can genuinely use.

People often talk too much about 'good saving habits' and don't pay enough attention to bad spending habits. Cure these, and the saving is much easier.

EACH MONTH THERE IS ALWAYS A LARGE EXPENSE WHICH TAKES UP MOST OF MY SAVINGS—HOW CAN I GET AHEAD?

Your budget will help you be aware of these big expenses and plan for them. It's much easier to put aside money for the car registration or phone bill each month than it is to find the money when the bill comes in. Try opening a separate account if you find yourself tempted to dip into this money each month. There are high-interest accounts (often Internet based) and cash management trusts which are a great place for these savings. Some have no minimum account balance or bank fees, and you can link them to your everyday bank account. You can even arrange for the money that you want to set aside to be automatically sent to this account each month, which removes the temptation for you to spend it.

WHAT'S YOUR SINGLE BEST TIP FOR SAVING?

Pay yourself first. Work out how much money you want to save each week or month and arrange for an automatic debit the moment your pay hits your bank account. Have the money transferred to a separate account before you've had time to spend it. That way you'll be forced to live on what you have left.

It sounds simple, but it's the reverse of what most people do. Most of us get paid and spend our money, intending to save what's left over. Problem is, that's usually nothing.

SMART TIP

HERE ARE 25 SAVING IDEAS TO GET YOU STARTED

1 Cutting out just one packet of cigarettes a week, or one or two drinks, will save as much as $10 a week.

2 Unless you've got the system rigged, gambling is money down the drain. Rethink your attitude to things like poker machines, scratchies and Lotto.

3 Take your lunch to work. Even doing this just one day a week will save money.

4 Takeaway and pre-packaged meals are expensive. Rediscover or discover the fun of cooking. Pasta and red wine with friends at home is cheap as well as fun.

5 Try to do your shopping in one go rather than continually dashing to the corner shop. Consider cheaper brands where you don't lose out on quality, and don't shop on an empty stomach.

6 Try cutting back to just the magazines you really can't live without. An avid book reader? Scour second-hand stores,

share with friends or join a local library to supplement your purchases.

7   Technology has made our lives much better, but it's also added to our expenses. Do you really need unlimited Internet access? Are you on a cost-efficient mobile phone plan? How often do you watch all the channels on Pay TV?

8   Are you using your phone cost-effectively and taking full advantage of the cheaper off-peak rates and other special offers?

9   Consider cheaper alternatives in entertainment. Maybe it's the movies that incur unexpected costs—why not rent a video one night a month instead?

10 Buying a second-hand car—rather than the new ego-driven model—can save heaps.

11 While we're talking about second-hand goods, are there other items you can buy that are pre-used? Scour the trash and treasure stores. A 1920s dress, or an old wooden table, can have heaps of style and cost a lot less than the latest offering from the retail stores.

12 Look at the auctions page in your newspaper. They can be fun as well as giving you access to cheap goods, and these days they sell everything from fine art to bathroom fittings.

13 Hunt around for sources of cheap entertainment. Does your local newspaper or radio station offer giveaway movie or theatre tickets? If all else fails, what about suggesting a picnic or walk on the beach to your friends instead of going out and spending a fortune?

14 What can you put off buying till the sales are on? Is there a cheap warehouse outlet or bargain centre where you can shop?

15 Club together with some friends to buy in bulk. Take turns to do your shopping at the fruit and vegie markets, where you can buy great fresh food at cheap prices.

16   Don't fall into the trap of false economy. One great item that will last for yonks is a better buy in the long run than something that's cheaper but wears out quickly or goes out of fashion within months.

17   Be gift smart. Become one of those painful people who buy gifts in advance, when they're on sale. By the time the Christmas rush comes around, you'll have a hoard of great presents that didn't cost the earth and you won't be forced into paying top dollar in a last-minute rush.

18   Cultivate a taste for water—yep, the stuff that comes out of the tap. When you think about the price you pay for soft drinks, you soon realise that old-fashioned H_2O can save big dollars over a year, and will probably leave you healthier. Many good cafes and bars now automatically provide filtered water to their customers at no charge. But steer clear of those dives that want to charge you just for turning on the tap.

19   Shop around. How many times have you bought something, only to see it at another shop—or worse still, in a friend's house—costing less? Check prices, scour the sales and the Internet, and ask your bargain-hunter friends where the best buys are. If you adopt the attitude that you're never going to pay full price again, finding cheaper items becomes a challenge.

20   Don't be afraid to negotiate. Ask whether you can get a better price on an item. Lots of stores will match competitors' prices (makes you wonder why they don't lower their prices anyway), so it always pays to ask whether a competitor has the item on sale. Many stores will also reduce the price if you ask for a discount—particularly if you're buying several items or a high-priced item like furniture or whitegoods. Bargaining doesn't have to be aggressive. Just ask politely, 'Can I get a discount because I'm buying three of these?'.

21 Use the Internet. While lots of goods are just as expensive on the Internet as buying retail—and that's before you add freight/postage—there are bargains to be found. Domestic airfares, for example, can almost always be found cheaper on the Net, and you can hunt around for the best fares yourself. Accommodation is another area where big savings can be found, especially if you want to book at the last minute. Lots of places offer cheap Web specials to fill their vacant rooms.

22 Use public transport when you can.

23 Look after your things. For example, make sure you keep up the maintenance on your car.

24 Avoid buying things on your credit card when you know you won't be able to pay it off in full at the end of the month. With credit card interest rates as much as 19 per cent, a $100 pair of jeans can end up costing you nearly $120 if you take a year to pay them off. If you really want something and you don't have the cash, ask the store whether they'll let you lay-by the goods instead.

25 Start swapping. If you're bored with your old books or CDs, swap them with some owned by a budget-conscious friend rather than going out and buying new ones.

THE PROBLEM IS MORE BASIC THAN THAT—I JUST DON'T EARN ENOUGH

What can you do to earn more? Can you take on a part-time job for a while? Work longer hours to earn overtime? Take on a flatmate or a boarder? Sell something? Lots of people overlook really simple ways of raising a bit of cash, such as selling your old books and CDs to a local second-hand store, holding a garage sale or selling some of your things through a stand at the local markets. People have raised $1000 or more through garage sales—getting rid of stuff they thought of as junk. It's not an ongoing income, but if you made a resolution to, say, hold a garage sale and use the money to pay off your credit card bill, it's a good step in getting you back on track.

MONEY ALERT

 Beware of those ads that offer big incomes through working at home. Many of them are just disguised pyramid schemes that rely on you recruiting other people to the network to earn money.

CHAPTER four

Another day older and deeper in debt—how to break the cycle

When our grandparents were young, it was much harder to borrow than it is today. If they wanted something, they saved up to buy it. It was as simple as that. These days we can borrow to buy just about anything, with no waiting at all. While this is good in the sense that we can live much better than our grandparents did, debt can be a real drag if you don't have control over it. So what do you need to know?

I THINK I'M ADDICTED TO PLASTIC—WHAT CAN I DO?

If you're constantly stretching the limits of your credit cards, and those offers of higher credit limits or a new card seem too good to be true, it's time for drastic action. Stop using the cards until every cent owing is paid off. Cut them up if you have to. Rest assured, they'll always give you a new one when you're back in control.

Tot up what you owe and budget to pay it off as fast as possible. Remember, you'll continue to be hit with those high interest rates until every cent is paid back.

You can use the marketing efforts of the card issuers to your advantage if you're prepared to be disciplined. Credit card issuers are constantly promoting their cards through offers such as 'Transfer money owing on your existing credit cards to our new card now and we'll give you a low interest rate for the first 12 months plus a heap of reward points'.

Take Suzi. She has around $3000 owing on her credit cards and is paying interest at around 19 per cent. If she takes advantage of one of these offers, Suzi can reduce her interest rate to less than 10 per cent and 'earn' 3000 reward points for her efforts. But to really make this worthwhile, Suzi should immediately cancel all her old cards and resolve not to use the new card until every cent is paid off.

If you're really in trouble with your credit cards, you could also consider debt consolidation. This is a strategy where you take out a personal loan at a lower interest rate to pay off all your credit card bills. Because the personal loan is structured to be paid off within a set period (usually two, three or five years), you are forced to reduce your debt, each month. But again, this only works if you're serious about breaking the habit. There's no point in debt consolidation if you're going to spend up big on your credit cards again.

When you've paid off your debts, think carefully about

how you'll avoid the same problem in the future. One idea is to limit yourself to just one credit card with a credit limit that you can manage. Or arrange a direct debit from your bank account each month to ensure that your account is repaid in full. If the money's not there to cover the payment, you'll be hit with dishonour fees, which is a big incentive to make sure you've got enough money set aside to cover the bill.

I LIKE THE CONVENIENCE OF CREDIT—CAN'T I BE SMARTER WITH CARDS INSTEAD OF GIVING THEM UP?

The first thing is to know exactly how the cards work. Generally there are two main types of credit cards on the market—ones which give you up to 55 interest-free days if you pay your bill by the due date each month, and ones where interest is charged immediately but at a lower interest rate. Both require a minimum payment each month, but this minimum payment often barely covers your interest bill. The cards are not structured to help you pay off your debt, and if you only make the minimum payment, it can take years to pay off your bill.

There are also two other types of cards that are often confused with credit cards, even though they're technically quite different.

Charge cards are offered by groups such as American Express and Diners Club. They look and feel just like ordinary credit cards—but there is one big difference. With a charge card your account must be paid in full each month. There is no ongoing credit and, if you don't meet a payment, hefty penalties can apply. Charge cards often have unlimited credit, so you can spend as much as you like—so long as you know you'll have the money to pay the bill at the end of each month.

Debit cards (also called ATM or EFTPOS cards) also look and feel like credit cards, but they don't actually give you any credit. They're linked to your bank account, so that when you spend money on your debit card, it's withdrawn directly from your account. A lot of people scoff at debit cards, partly because you're using your own money and partly because they don't usually give you reward points. But look at their advantages: you can't get into debt for things you can't afford, and there are no high interest rates. For those who like the convenience of credit cards, but have trouble managing them, debit cards are a much better choice.

MONEY ALERT

Read very carefully with those offers to 'Buy now with no repayments until 2010' (or thereabouts). They're a sucker play to get you to buy things you can't afford. Too often people sign up, and then find at the end of the no-repayment period that they still don't have the money to pay for this purchase. They then get slugged with high interest rates on the debt.

HOW DO I CHOOSE A CREDIT CARD THAT SUITS ME?

The first question to ask yourself (and answer honestly!) is: Do I pay less than the full amount due on my credit card most months? The second question: Do I ever get cash advances on my credit card?

If the answer to either of these questions is yes, you should think seriously about getting a debit card or a credit card with no interest-free period. Your key objective should be to find the card with the lowest possible interest rate.

What many people don't realise is that not paying your bill in full, or getting cash advances, wipes out many of the benefits of credit cards with interest-free days.

Why is that? Interest on cash advances kicks in immediately. There's no interest-free period, so you're paying that higher interest rate from the minute the cash is in your hot little hand. To add insult to injury, there's often a transaction fee for the cash advance too.

'That's okay,' I hear you say. 'I only want the cash advance to tide me over until pay day. Two days' interest isn't going to break the bank.' But there's another catch. You can't elect to pay off the cash advance and leave your other purchases unpaid. The banks calculate these things so that your repayment is applied automatically to any earlier purchases. Let's say you'd already spent $500 on your card. You get a $200 cash advance today, and go to your bank tomorrow with $200 to repay it. No go. The $200 will go towards repaying your previous purchases, so you end up owing $300 on your purchases and with the $200 cash advance still outstanding. You'd have to take in the full $700 to ensure that your cash advance was paid off.

Banks use a similar trick when you don't pay off your entire credit card balance before the due date. This is because the interest-free period only applies if you pay your card bill in full. If you don't, interest kicks in—and it can be backdated. Instead of just being charged interest on the amount still outstanding after the due date (which seems the logical thing to do), some banks backdate the interest to the date of purchase. This happens even if you pay off most of your bill but leave only a small amount—even $1—outstanding.

Some credit card providers backdate only to the date of your statement, which is better. And some, better still, only charge interest on the amount outstanding after your repayment (if you pay part of the bill by the due date).

But it gets worse. If you are caught paying interest, some providers charge interest on all purchases that have been debited to your account—whether they appeared on your statement or were transacted after the statement was issued. If this is the case, you will have to pay the total amount outstanding on your card—not just the amount on your statement—to regain your interest-free status.

I LIKE THE IDEA OF SOMETHING FREE FOR MY SPENDING—WHAT ABOUT REWARD POINTS?

Reward points should be considered as a bonus—getting a lot of points for air travel or other things is not a good reason to select the wrong card. Even if you spend a lot on your credit cards, the 'rewards' are marginal—there should be a bonus if they're available, but not if that means you are paying high annual fees or a high interest rate with no interest-free period.

If you really want a card with reward points, choose one that suits your spending patterns and the rewards you want. Some cards have partnership arrangements where you can earn bonus points if you spend with the partner. If you regularly shop at the same places, and can earn bonus points from doing so, this is a consideration.

If you're looking for rewards to supplement your frequent flyer points, your reward points must be able to be converted into frequent flyer points—preferably at one point per dollar spent.

Most cards offer rewards of goods and services ranging from hotel stays to gift vouchers to products offered by bonus partners.

Also look for a scheme where your reward points have no expiry date or at least last for a long time—particularly if you look like being slow in building up the points.

I'VE JUST LEFT UNI AND STARTED MY FIRST JOB—WHEN DO I HAVE TO REPAY MY STUDENT LOAN?

You don't have to start repayments until you reach a minimum level of income—$15 964 p.a. (or $307 per week).

Note that all income is counted, not just wages or salary. Dividends, interest, trust distributions, rents, etc. are considered to be part of your income. Once your income reaches the Student Loan threshold, the Internal Revenue Department (IRD) calculates your repayments. As soon as you are earning over this amount you have to pay 10 per cent of your income as repayments. In most cases your employer will deduct money for your student loan from your pay on a regular basis. You should tell your employer to use the SL tax code. If you are earning less than the threshold amount you do not have to make repayments but don't forget that the loan continues to attract interest.

The IRD has the authority to apply penalties if you breach the terms of the loan. If you fail to make the payments on time you can be charged a penalty of 2 per cent per month on the outstanding amount. This penalty compounds—you will pay interest on the interest if you don't make your repayments! This can get out of control rapidly—and apart from the financial implications it is not a good record for you to have.

For further details you should check out the IRD Website at www.ird.govt.nz. There is a student loan calculator on the site and lots of detailed and interesting information. The IRD can be called on 0800 377778. It is never a good idea to try to provoke the IRD—they have far-reaching powers and they will pursue you relentlessly. They are bigger and brighter than any individual and they take their revenue collection responsibilities on behalf of the government very seriously!

There is also a very useful book called *Get Rid of Your Student Loan* by Lisa Schultz (Random House, 2002) and a corresponding Website, www.student-loan.co.nz.

WHAT IF I WANT TO GO ON MY OE?

Many young people are anxious to get overseas to begin the big OE. Others may be tempted to disappear overseas to avoid their loan repayments. The terms of the student loan scheme require that repayments and all of the other conditions still apply if you are overseas. Furthermore, if you are going abroad for longer than three months you are required to contact the IRD and give them your overseas address. They will continue to calculate payments and you must make the repayments every three months.

The IRD have a useful booklet called *Going Overseas* that will give you all the details you need to decide if that's a good option right now and how to continue to manage your student loan debt while overseas.

If you are committed to going overseas it may be advisable to visit an IRD office and discuss your circumstances. If you will not be earning much (or anything at all!) while overseas you may be able to arrange a low payment regime.

On the other hand, going overseas may be a deliberate tactic to earn valuable foreign currency—if you have good skills and are going to a high-wage economy like the United Kingdom or the United States you may be able to save significant money that you can use to repay your debt fast. Many educated and skilled Kiwis seem to be taking this option. If you choose this path you would do best to devote as much as you can save to additional repayments on your loan.

I WANT TO REDUCE MY STUDENT LOAN DEBT AS FAST AS POSSIBLE— SHOULD I PAY IT OFF NOW OR JUST KEEP HAVING IT TAKEN OUT OF MY SALARY?

You will be better off repaying your student loan debt as soon as you can. The interest rate is quite high (around 7 per cent) and the debt is not tax deductible. Any spare money you have should be used to reduce the loan as much as you can and as quickly as possible. It makes no sense 'saving' or investing money elsewhere as long as you have this loan—you would have to be getting very high returns before it was a better financial deal than repaying your loan. If you are lucky enough to get a gift, a bonus at work, a distribution from a trust or a pay increase you should put it towards the repayment of your loan. You can pay off the student loan in whole or in part at any time, even when you are still a student—if you were lucky enough to receive an inheritance, for example. (While you are still a student the student loan scheme is administered by WINZ. You can contact the Student Services Centre (part of WINZ) on 0800 889900 or access the Website at www.winz. govt.nz.)

HOW DO I KNOW WHAT THE BEST REPAYMENT OPTIONS ARE?

You can work out how much you owe and the best repayment options using an online calculator. Go to www.student-loan.co.nz or www.ird.govt.nz. The IRD will also run these calculations for you if you have no online access.

You can check out how much you currently owe, how much interest you will pay in total, when your last repayment will be, what will happen to your debt if you fail to make payments and most importantly you can explore the effect of making additional repayments. People are often staggered by the effect of making a large one-off repayment or the impact of increasing the amount of your regular repayments. The total interest that you pay will reduce significantly as will the duration of the debt—leaving you free to begin saving and investing in other assets.

I CAN'T PAY OFF MY CARDS, STUDENT LOAN AND CAR LOAN AT ONCE— WHERE SHOULD I START?

Here's one of those basic rules of money management that sounds so obvious you'd think even a two-year-old could work it out: you pay off the most expensive debts first. Look at your loans, compare the interest rate and any other costs on each, work out which one is costing you the most, and concentrate on getting rid of it. Once it's paid off, you can then turn your attention to paying off the debt with the second-highest rate, and so on.

You have no choice about addressing your student loan debt—it's a requirement of the Student Loan scheme that you make repayments as soon as you reach the income threshold of $15 964 p.a.—and you have to pay 10 per cent of your income towards repayments. However, you have choices about whether you pay more or not. You should make that choice based on the cost of the various debts you have.

In most cases, it's the high-interest credit card debt that's the big expense. But if you only owe, say $1000 on your credit card, and you owe $10 000 on your car loan, it's easy to think that the car loan is costing you more, as the repayments are higher. However, for each dollar borrowed, this is a much cheaper debt.

It's important to understand this concept of cheap versus expensive debt before you buy your own home. We often see people ploughing every extra dollar they have into paying off their mortgage, which has an interest rate of around 7 per cent, while running up debts on their credit cards and paying interest at 19 per cent. They concentrate on the mortgage because it's big—huge, in fact. But they'd actually have more money available to reduce the mortgage if they got rid of those expensive credit card debts first.

SMART TIP

Financial advisers talk about good debt and bad debt. The good debts are the loans you take out to buy things that will hold or increase their value—such as your home or investments. It's not so bad paying interest on these items, as they're always going to be worth at least what you paid for them; with any luck, they'll soon be worth more.

Bad debts are debts over things that fall in value—like most cars, consumer goods or holidays (which don't have any monetary value at all once you've taken them). With bad debts, you're paying interest on something that isn't even worth what you paid for it. And to cap it off, bad debts usually carry higher interest rates than good debts.

IF I HAVEN'T ALREADY GOT A STUDENT LOAN SHOULD I TAKE ONE OUT?

You may well be considering further education and wondering if you should take on the burden of a student loan. Many young people (and their families) are very concerned about incurring such a debt—they worry that it will take years to repay and wonder if it is worth it. We would say that the real issue is whether an education is worth the trouble. The overwhelming evidence is that education is financially advantageous to the individual. Obviously, each case is different but generally every extra year of education pays off financially—and it does that for your whole life! (And that is only the financial benefit—there are many other payoffs as well.)

A Student Loan is a good debt because you are borrowing to build an asset—you! You are your own most important asset and you should therefore invest in yourself. In that sense, a student loan is an investment in your future earning capacity and is one that should repay you several times over.

While the amounts can look daunting (the average student loan debt in NZ is between $15 000 and $20 000—you need to think of the value of this investment over the 30, 40 or 50 years that you may be earning well as a consequence of your education. And while no one can guarantee you employment, you will increase your employability and income-producing capacity with further education—you are able to do more, you can learn new things more easily, you have a proven record of achievement. These attributes will be of value all of your life, which should give you a very good return on your investment.

Even though there is a great deal of coverage in the NZ media about the size and burden of student loans it pays to remember that education in NZ is priced cheaply compared to the rest of the OECD—in other words, you get a lot for your money if you 'buy' an education in NZ.

SHOULD I TAKE OUT A LOAN EVEN IF I DON'T NEED THE MONEY?

Many students don't need to take out a loan while studying— they are supported by their parents or they may have saved enough from working before becoming a student or they may even continue to earn as a student. Because most students don't pay interest on the loan while still a student some choose to take the interest-free money and invest it. This means that they earn interest on the government's money—at no cost to themselves! Some have used it to purchase a house. Financially this is straightforward and legal. However, if you choose this option be careful that you invest safely and that you repay the loan as soon as you can.

I GOT INTO TROUBLE WITH MY CREDIT CARDS A FEW YEARS BACK— HAS THIS AFFECTED MY CREDIT RATING?

It probably has, though if it was an isolated example, and you've met all your repayments since then, you should still be able to borrow without too much trouble. Credit information about you is kept by various credit reporting agencies such as Baycorp Advantage and RMG. Every time you apply for credit, the lender can look up your file to check your credit record. The agencies make their money by selling credit information to lenders. You are entitled to contact these agencies and ask for any records that they have on you so that you can check them for accuracy. The credit reporting agencies must supply you with a copy of their records on you within 21 days. It is worth checking what data they hold, especially if you have a common name and think that there may be some confusion with someone else. As well as keeping records of when you applied for or inquired about finance, credit agencies also keep records of court judgments and bankruptcies and, more importantly in cases like this, details of seriously overdue accounts and those which have been settled or brought up to date.

If you've had a problem in the past, your best bet is to be upfront about it when you're applying for a new loan. Disclose the problem, and tell the lender how it was settled. The odds are they'll find out about it anyway, and non-disclosure would be a further black mark.

If you are refused credit on the basis of information received from the agency, the lender will advise you of the fact and recommend that you get a copy of your file. You should take that advice and take steps to improve your credit rating as soon as possible.

SMART TIP

Don't wait to find out whether there is any dirt on you. You are entitled to get a copy of any records that they hold on you within 21 days of request. Write to Baycorp at PO Box 90845, Auckland or call them on 0800 229267.

I JUST CAN'T REPAY MY DEBTS—WHO CAN I TURN TO FOR HELP?

Many community organisations offer help to people who are struggling with debt. Your local Citizens Advice Bureau is a good place to start. They can provide some expertise or refer you to other experts. There is a network of Budget Advice Services around the country—see your local phone book.

You could also consider using a financial adviser. That is likely to be more expensive but depending on your circumstances and your longer-term goals it may be a good option. The best way to find a good adviser is to ask people you trust for a recommendation. The Financial Planners and Insurers Association (FPIA) will have a list of members in your area. They can be accessed at www.fpia.org.nz. For lists of planners by geographical area see www.good returns.co.nz.

IS BANKRUPTCY AN OPTION?

It's a last resort. Your financial and personal future will be greatly affected by the declaration of bankruptcy. For example, you are not allowed to travel overseas, take on any debt or manage a company for at least three years after declaring bankruptcy without the permission of the Official Assignee. So while bankruptcy is an option, it is not one to be taken lightly.

If you are facing the prospect of bankruptcy, get some good advice and explore any options you have to avoid a declaration of bankruptcy. Options might include selling any assets you can or renegotiating with your creditors so that you can pay off your debts more slowly at a level you can manage.

Bankruptcy gives you immediate relief from all your debts. However, you will only be allowed to keep personal effects to the value of $2000 and cash of $400. Everything else will be taken to pay off your debts (you are allowed to keep the tools of your trade, if you have one, but only to the value of $500).

All that is bad enough but the real effects are in the future—the credit rating agencies will have your bankruptcy on record and it will affect both your ability to borrow and, in many cases, your employment.

There is good information on the law concerning bankruptcy and its effects at the Website of the New Zealand Insolvency and Trustee Services (www.insolvency.govt.nz).

CHAPTER five

Banks are bastards—
but you can beat them

Just running your day-to-day finances can seem like a real chore these days. There are so many bank accounts on the market and they all seem to have different ways of sticking their hands in your pocket. My theory is that the banks don't want people to understand their products, because if we did, most of us would be downright furious. So what do you need to know to bring the bastards to account?

HOW AM I SUPPOSED TO GET AHEAD WHEN I'M LOSING SO MUCH MONEY EACH MONTH IN BANK FEES?

Good question. My first suggestion is to put the problem back on your bank. It's the banks who have developed all these complicated fee structures, and yet they're the ones who go around saying customers should use their accounts smarter so they pay less in fees. So ask them to do the hard work for you. Look at your bank statements from the past three or six months and work out your average and minimum monthly balances and the average number of each type of transactions you make each month—branch withdrawals and deposits, direct debits, cheque withdrawals and deposits, Internet transfers, EFTPOS withdrawals and so on. Take the list to your bank and ask them to suggest ways you could organise your money better. (Yes, I know this approach means actually looking at your bank statements, not just tossing them into a drawer. But how do you expect the banks to take your fee gripe seriously if you don't even know your own banking habits?)

Put the hard word on your bank to suggest the most cost-effective account for you. If you are a heavy account user, it may be better to pay a higher account-keeping fee for an account with unlimited or a high number of free transactions. Or, if you do most of your transactions using ATMs, EFTPOS and phone or Internet banking, you might be better with an account that has high fees for over-the-counter service but low fees for electronic transactions. For all the talk in recent years about low-cost 'basic' bank accounts, many of the cheap offerings available are restricted to people like pensioners, and are not much good for the average wage earner. But all the major banks have an array of options, and chances are, there's one that will suit you.

HOW DO I FIND OUT IF THE BANK FEES I'M PAYING ARE TOO HIGH?

You will have to do a bit of analysis to work this out—there is no 'right' fee as it all depends of what kinds of activity you conduct with your bank. Banks charge for just about everything they do nowadays—after all, they are a business, not a public service! You should ask what the different services you use cost and unless you really need those services you should avoid using them. It is very hard to manage your bank fees if you are not aware what you are charged for each activity. Banking in New Zealand is very competitive as there are many banks. Some such as the Taranaki Savings Bank (TSB) and Kiwibank have very attractive rates but may have more limited offerings than other banks. You do need to shop around and get the fee structure that suits your needs best. Be mindful of your time and energies however: the same effort invested in earning you more might give you a better return on your time than chasing the last dollar reduction in your bank fees!

MY BANK HAS A FEE REBATE SYSTEM—IS THAT A BETTER DEAL?

To our minds, it's another way of muddying the picture so that the average person doesn't have a clue what they're actually paying. Rebate systems vary, but the idea is that you're given a rebate or allowance each month that is offset against bank fees.

IS THERE ANY WAY I CAN GET OUT OF PAYING FEES ALTOGETHER?

Many banks offer fee-free accounts to groups such as students, pensioners and home loan customers. But surprise, surprise— as often as not you have to ask whether they have them. They're not what you'd call pro-active about promoting the fact. If you qualify for a banking 'package', which generally requires you to have a set amount of business with the bank, you may also get a fee-free account. Many banks now offer what they call 'relationship' packages for groups such as professionals or other customers who put lots of money their way. Packages vary, but they generally offer discounts on banking services, bonus interest rates on products such as term deposits, fee-free transaction accounts and credit cards— and often investment management, insurance and other financial services offered by the banking group. In isolation, the discounts don't amount to much—especially when you consider that the banks can charge several hundred dollars for these packages. Some packages also require you to have large sums of money on deposit—so large that often the last place you would want to put the money is in a lazy bank account.

But the real thrust is to persuade you to put all your business with the bank and get the discounts on a wide range of financial services. Our advice is to negotiate—always ask for fee reductions. Research tends to indicate that we are very poor at asking for discounts but often asking is all we need to do.

DO I NEED A CHEQUE ACCOUNT?

Now that you can transfer money to anyone's account using Internet banking, it's easier to live without a cheque book. Chances are you can pay most of your regular major bills online or by direct debit. For the rare case that you need a cheque, you can easily buy a bank cheque.

If you really feel you have to have a cheque account, one alternative is to have a separate cheque account that you only use for the money you need to write cheques. That way you can keep most of your money in a different account; one that pays a better rate of interest. But try to avoid having too many accounts as you'll probably end up doubling up on account-keeping fees too.

SMART TIP

HERE ARE EIGHT TIPS TO REDUCE BANK FEES

1   Find out how your bank counts your transactions. Some start with the most expensive transactions each month and include these in your fee-free limit, and others operate on a first-in, first-counted basis so you could end up getting the cheap transactions for free and paying for the expensive ones.

2   Try to use cheaper electronic transactions such as ATMs, phone, EFTPOS or the Internet rather than going into the bank branch. But keep a record of phone and Internet transactions in case there's a dispute.

3   Avoid using ATMs that don't belong to your own bank. The banks call them 'foreign' ATMs and charge you for the plane ticket they clearly think they need to transfer the money.

4   If you use EFTPOS for purchases, take out any cash you need at the same time. That's two transactions for the price of one.

5   Don't be an ATM junkie. Take out as much money as you need from your pay and then leave the ATM card at home. It helps your budgeting and stops you making small withdrawals every time you decide to go out for coffee.

6   If you've managed to get on top of your credit card, consider using it for paying bills and making purchases. That way you can take advantage of the interest-free period and pay the credit card bill as just one transaction at the end of the month. But remember, this only works if you're disciplined enough to pay your credit card off in full before the due date.

7   Consider maintaining the minimum account balance required to avoid account-keeping fees.

8 Organise for your bills to be automatically deducted from your bank account. That's called a direct debit.

IS THERE AN ACCOUNT THAT PAYS A REASONABLE INTEREST RATE ON A SMALL AMOUNT OF SAVINGS?

If you've got at least $500 (or preferably $1000), a cash management trust is an option. These are a type of investment product, rather than a bank account. They pool your money along with that of a lot of other investors and place it in the professional money market. Unlike bank accounts, you get market interest rates (minus management fees of about 1 per cent), which makes them a much more serious savings proposition. On the whole, you get paid about 1 per cent more of interest than a bank account. But they're less flexible than bank accounts and are often not suited to people making a lot of transactions. UDC, AXA and Macquarie Group all offer such products paying higher interest rates.

If you're prepared to lock your savings away for a while, however, it might be worth looking at a term deposit. These pay you a set rate of interest for a fixed period (it could be a month, or it could be five years) and can often give you a better return than an ordinary bank account. But don't stick your money in a term deposit if you know you have a big bill coming up—it's hard to break the term deposit and, if you do, you'll generally lose your interest.

INTEREST RATES SEEM TO CHANGE ALL THE TIME—HOW DO I FIND OUT WHO HAS THE BEST CURRENT RATES?

Most major newspapers now publish tables showing who has the best rates in the business or personal finance sections. The Website at www.goodreturns.co.nz allows you to search for the rates on offer—for example, who is offering what rates on $1000 deposited for one month? Newspapers are also full of ads from financial companies and banks promoting their latest interest rate offerings. Beware, however, of chasing the highest return and putting your money at risk—some of the companies that offer to pay very high interest rates may be quite small and not very stable or strong. Such companies do sometimes go broke. It makes no sense to get a high interest rate but end up losing your money.

CHAPTER six
Funny money—how to enjoy life without breaking the bank

It often seems the world is made up of two financial types. One is the spendthrift who buys everything he fancies and is constantly in debt. And the other is the financial bore who knows exactly where every cent she has ever earned has gone. There's got to be a happy medium!

This chapter looks at what you need to know to ensure that your lifestyle purchases are smart ones.

WHAT'S THE BEST WAY TO BUY A NEW CAR?

Work out what you want and then shop around. Successful car dealers have boasted that most people come out of car dealerships with a car they didn't know they wanted. That's great salesmanship, but for young people wanting to get on top of their finances, it can also mean spending too much on something you don't really need.

The solution is to know what you want beforehand, and what you should pay, then refuse to be diverted from your chosen path. Questions to ask include:

- How far will I be driving the car? Comfort and oomph are more important if you're driving long distances than if you merely want something in which to zip around your local area.
- How many passengers or goods will I be carrying? How big does my car need to be?
- What's the car's fuel consumption? A petrol guzzler is a huge drain on anyone's budget. The Consumers' Institute has data on the fuel efficiency of various models. You can access this online for free if you are an online member or you can purchase a membership for three months for $20 (three months ought to be long enough to find your car).
- How much ego do I have at stake here? Do I need a car that boasts about who I am or can I make a statement by driving something more economical?
- What's the resale value on this model? How well does it hold its value?
- How safe is the car?
- How much will it cost to run the car? Most people don't realise that even a small car eats up more than $100 a week. The Website at www.consumer.org.nz has lots of other useful reports such as '5 Steps to Buying a Car', a 'Car

Inspection Checklist', 'Car Buyer's Rights' and a 'Car Reliability Report'. A $20 online subscription looks worthwhile given the amount you will be spending. You can also call them on 0800 CONSUMER and get hard-copy reports for a small fee.

SHOULD I BUY NEW OR SECOND-HAND?

You should usually buy second-hand. All else being equal, you should not buy something that loses a big chunk of its value the minute you drive it out of the dealer's yard. That's what happens when you buy a new car; the minute you take ownership of it, it becomes a used car and worth less. People like to buy new cars because they think they're problem free, and that's usually true. However, there are, unfortunately, some cars that are poorly made to start with—although you are less likely to be buying someone else's problem than you are with a used car.

ISN'T IT BETTER TO GET A NEW CAR WITH A WARRANTY?

It's one way of guarding against ending up with a lemon, and some of the warranties that have been offered in recent years are worth considering. Some dealers of new cars, for example, have offered warranties for as long as five years.

While dealers will also offer a warranty on second-hand cars, they are rarely this generous. A used-car warranty will be for a shorter period and it may not cover everything that was covered when the car was new. Another option is to buy mechanical failure insurance. This covers the failure of any part of your engine, transmission or differential drive. This type of insurance tends to be restricted, though—you may not be able to get it if your car is older or has lots of Ks on the clock.

SMART TIP

The best place to get a quick idea of what a car is worth is in your local newspapers—because so many are traded frequently you can get a fairly accurate picture of what each model is worth given its age, mileage and condition.

Another favourite way is to take it to one of the numerous car auctions around NZ. The organisers will give you an estimate of what it will sell for—and they are fairly accurate.

I'M TERRIFIED OF GETTING RIPPED OFF—WHAT CAN I DO?
The Automobile Association (AA) will do an inspection of your prospective purchase for a fee. But you obviously don't want to pay this until you're pretty sure you've found the car you want. If you don't have a tame, mechanically minded mate to take along on your car hunt, there are some basic checks you can do yourself to spot any obvious problems.

First up, have a good look at the car in the sunlight. Are there any signs that it has been damaged or patched up? Is there any rust or shoddy paintwork? Colour differences? Does it look the way you'd expect a well-maintained car to look? *Choice* (an Aussie consumer magazine) suggests you keep a fridge magnet in your pocket and check suspicious-looking areas for body filler. If the magnet won't stick, there's filler under the paintwork. It's a good tip!

Turn the engine on and let the car idle. Is it running smoothly or are there funny noises? Is the exhaust giving off fumes or making a racket?

Taking the car for a test drive is the easy bit. It's a good idea to drive through streets where you stop and start frequently as well as on open roads. How does it handle the hills? Does it corner smoothly? Pump the brakes a few times—how fast do they respond? How does the suspension feel? Is it a smooth ride or do you feel every bump? What about the gear changes? Are they smooth? If the car is an automatic, do the gears change as you'd expect them to? Stop the car and hop out for a few minutes. Does it restart without any problems? Do the locks, doors, windows, wipers, heater, fan, lights, sound system and so on all work as they should? How are the tyres? Are they wearing evenly or is there extra wear in one area? This can indicate problems with the suspension or steering.

If you're buying second-hand, you should also ask to see the car's maintenance records. Has it been serviced regularly? If it has, there's less chance of a major problem. What work has been done in recent years and what has it cost? Has the mechanic made any notes on the report about upcoming work that will be needed?

All of these aspects can seem quite technical to someone who knows little about cars so if at all possible, ask a friend who is knowledgeable about cars and who has bought and sold several to accompany you.

If all this checks out, you can feel more confident about getting a professional in for that final check.

MONEY ALERT

If you buy a stolen car, it can be reclaimed by its owner without you getting back the money you paid for it. And if you buy a car and there's still money owing on it you will be responsible for paying it back. Since the *Personal Properties Securities Act* came into force in May 2002 there is an online register where you can check the security on any item you are buying. The Website is at www.ppsr.govt.nz.

When you are buying privately you should also check that all of the paperwork is correct—that the person selling the car is the registered owner, and that the engine and vehicle identification numbers on the car match those on the registration papers.

AM I BETTER OFF BUYING MY SECOND-HAND CAR THROUGH A DEALER OR PRIVATELY?

There's no hard-and-fast rule. Dealers have to comply with warranty regulations and, if you have an old car to trade in, can often be the simpler alternative. But buying privately may be cheaper, as you're cutting out the middle man.

However, if you buy from a dealer both the *Fair Trading Act* and the *Consumer Guarantees Act* apply to the transaction which gives you considerable protection. You will also have some protection under the *Motor Vehicle Dealers Act*. If you buy privately you are on your own and have little means of redress if you make a very poor choice. One of the things that you can check out quickly and cheaply is whether any money is owed on the car. (It will cost you $5 plus GST to call Autocheck on 0900 90977 to ensure that the car you are considering is fully owned by the vendor—otherwise you may be buying a great deal of trouble for yourself.)

Another alternative is car auctions. Look out for them in your local paper. The advantage of these is that you can get great bargains; the downside is that you may not be able to take the car for a test drive, and you have to make a fast decision at the auction—you can't time the purchase to suit yourself. Some of the better auctioneers are now offering cars with inspections already completed by the relevant motoring organisation and some cars sold at auction come with warranties. If you're thinking of buying at auction, get your finances together before you go. Most auctioneers require you to make a sizeable deposit once your bid is successful, and to pay the full amount within 24 hours.

MONEY ALERT

A common trick used by dealers is to advertise cheap deals and then, once you've decided to buy, increase their profit margin by selling you lots of extras. And once you've made the decision to spend thousands of dollars, it's really easy to get sucked into spending a bit more. The more features you can get as 'standard' the better, and don't pay for extra things you really don't need.

WHAT'S THE BEST WAY TO FINANCE MY NEW CAR?

Try cash. Seriously. Remember in Chapter 4 when we talked about different kinds of debt? Car loans in any shape or form are bad debts because most cars—new cars especially—are worth less than you paid the minute you drive off in them. Cars are depreciating assets—which means the longer you own them, the less they're worth. You should adopt a policy of borrowing only to buy things that appreciate in value (e.g., real estate).

In an ideal world, no one would borrow to buy a car. We'd all save up, use cash, and only buy what we could afford. But life isn't perfect and the fact is that most of us need a car to get around. For many people, that means you have to borrow.

Dealer-arranged finance is almost always more expensive than other types of finance, so talk to your bank, and shop around for finance before you commit yourself to a purchase. Most borrowers now use special car loans—personal loans that are secured against your car. If you don't meet the repayments, the lender can repossess your car. But the interest rate is generally okay and these loans are structured so that you pay the car off in a fixed period—such as five years. One problem with car loans is that they may only be available for new cars, or newer second-hand vehicles. If your new car doesn't fit into the lending requirements, you may need to look at a slightly more expensive unsecured personal loan. Another alternative if you have to borrow for a car is to put it on your home loan. This is the cheapest source of finance but you should be sure to increase your mortgage payments by the amount that you would have paid for a hire purchase deal.

WHAT ABOUT CAR LEASING? IS THAT A BETTER DEAL?

Leasing is a totally different proposition from buying a car and taking out a loan to pay for it. That's because when you lease a car, you don't actually own it. It is owned by the finance company that provides the lease and you pay for the use of the car.

Let's say you agree with a dealer to buy a $10 000 car under a lease arrangement. The dealer sells the car to the finance company for $10 000. You agree to a lease agreement that gives you the right to use the car for a set period, such as 36 months. Your lease agreement will set out two key figures. The first is the monthly payment you're required to make, and the second is the 'balloon' or 'residual'. Think of this as the value of the car after it has been depreciated (or written down in value) over the three years in which you used it.

Your monthly payments cover the depreciation of the car plus interest, but you'll find finance companies are keen to wrap these up into a single figure. This way, the monthly repayments appear lower than they would on a loan to buy the car and you think you're getting a great deal. But that's because you're only paying for the use of the car, not to own it. It's important to find out what the interest rate actually is to work out whether or not it's really a good deal. At the end of the lease period, some types of leases allow you to simply give the car back to the leasing company. In other types of leases, you may be able to buy it from the leasing company or use it as a trade-in on a new car. One catch with many standard leases is that if the car is worth less than the residual at the end of the lease term, you'll be asked to make up the difference.

MONEY ALERT

Make sure your new car is insured before you drive it anywhere! The last thing you want is to have an accident on the way home and then remember that you're not covered.

I LIVE IN A SHARED HOUSE AND WE ARGUE ABOUT MONEY—WHAT'S THE BEST WAY TO HANDLE SHARED FINANCES?

Money arguments can be one of the worst things about sharing—and in every household there always seems to be at least one person who's always broke when there's a big bill to be paid. One solution is to budget for costs like electricity and phone bills and incorporate them into the regular rent payments. You can put this money into a special savings account so that, by the time the bill arrives, you have most of the money needed to cover it.

Itemised phone bills have overcome many of the problems of who spent what, but if you're still having problems with your phone bill, you could consider getting a toll bar on the phone so that it can only be used for local calls. Another option, if you have a mobile phone, is to skip the fixed line altogether and be responsible for your own phone costs.

Each household develops its own system for handling money, but your best strategy is to make sure you're sharing with people who think like you do. If you're the only person in the household who is budget-conscious, the odds are you'll end up unhappy and out of pocket.

One of the obligations that is easily overlooked when sharing a house are those attaching to your lease. Often in shared accommodation there is a great deal of movement—people come and go frequently, different people move in and out, the group who are sharing the rent and expenses changes. If you are the person who signed the lease your responsibilities continue even if you move out. Make sure that if you are moving out you notify the landlord and get the responsibilities transferred to those staying behind—you don't want your name on the lease when the consequences of a major party months later are being followed up!

Sometimes one person signs the lease and invites other flatmates to join and share expenses. You would be in a much better position if all of the flatmates signed the lease agreement so that responsibility is shared—that way it is in everyone's interest to take care of the rented property and to ensure that visitors do likewise.

MY LANDLORD NEVER DOES REPAIRS WHEN I ASK FOR THEM—WHAT ARE MY RIGHTS?

In return for you paying your bond, looking after the property and paying your rent on time, your landlord is required to keep the property in a reasonable state of repair. Generally, your landlord is required to ensure that the premises are fit to live in and to organise any urgent repairs—such as fixing burst pipes, a broken loo, an electrical fault or a gas leak—as soon as reasonably possible. They're also required to fix any problem that makes the premises unsafe or not secure. That doesn't mean your landlord has to fix every little problem that crops up, but it does mean they should fix problems that endanger you or prevent you from living reasonably comfortably in the property.

If your landlord is tardy about fixing problems, you should put your request in writing. If that doesn't work, apply to the Government agency that looks after tenants, Tenancy Services (a division of the Ministry of Housing), to order your landlord to do the work. Tenancy Services produce a number of excellent booklets, full of advice and tips, and you can contact them at www.tenancy.co.nz or on 0800 836262.

MY PARTNER WANTS US TO MOVE IN TOGETHER, BUT THEY'RE HOPELESS WITH MONEY—WHAT SHOULD I DO TO PROTECT MYSELF?

You've actually got a head start on a lot of couples because you recognise a potential problem. All too often it's only after people move in together that they realise they speak different financial languages. The *Property (Relationships) Act* came into effect in 2002 and has greatly changed the law regarding property and relationships.

The first thing to do is to sit down and talk about how you'll manage your money together. The good news is that it's generally cheaper to live with someone else than by yourself, so start by identifying areas you'll save money—like rent. Then come to an agreement on who should pay what, and what you're going to do with your savings.

If you're renting, whose name will the lease be in? Ditto for the electricity, phone and gas accounts. It makes sense to have them in both names, but this means that you are what's known as 'jointly and severally liable' for the bills. That means that if your partner gets into financial strife and can't pay their share, your landlord or the phone company can chase you for the money. If this is a potential problem, maybe you should consider putting some of the accounts in your name and others in theirs.

What about joint purchases? At the moment you both own your own things and will use them together. But what happens when you need a new lounge suite or DVD player? One option is to set up a special joint savings account for these sorts of purchases. Alternatively, you could agree for one of you to buy it independently and keep it if the relationship breaks up. If your partner is a worry with money, it's dangerous for you to take out a joint loan or credit card with them to buy these sorts of items because you could end up paying for them all by yourself—or ending up with a black mark on your credit rating because you couldn't repay the loan. And what's worse, if there's no record of who paid what you could find your ex demanding the new lounge suite if you break up. In fact, if you're worried about your partner's money management skills, be very careful about signing any loan agreements or guarantees in which your partner's involved. That 'joint and severally liable' clause can bite you there too.

Of course, if this is a longer-term relationship (over three years), it will be covered by the *Property (Relationships) Act.* If one of you has more assets than the other, perhaps you should agree to list what you're both bringing into the relationship so there are no arguments later about who owns what. This isn't the same as a formal property sharing agreement, but it's better than nothing. A formal property sharing agreement will cost you as you both have to get advice from a lawyer. If there is a significant amount of assets at stake, you should discuss this with your partner and get good advice.

There's no need to rush into things like joint bank accounts and credit cards. In fact many long-married couples still prefer to keep these personal finance details separate so they don't have silly arguments over who spent what.

But you can think about insurance. There are some sorts of insurance—such as contents insurance—that you can combine. You may also want to consider income protection insurance, which pays you an income if you're unable to work because of sickness or an accident, now that someone else is partly relying on your ability to earn an income.

If the relationship looks like getting really serious, it's also worth talking now about some of the issues that may crop up in the future. Do you have the same financial dreams and objectives? It sounds crass, but many a relationship has gone off the rails because he's dreaming of a new sports car and she wants a home of her own; or she's set on making her fortune and he fancies growing vegetables and body hair in the country. Do you want to buy a home together? If you do, what sort of home do you want and how will you jointly save for it? What about children? You don't have to make a detailed plan for your whole life, but you do need to agree on joint financial goals and how you'll work towards them.

SMART TIP

HERE ARE 10 THINGS YOU MUST KNOW ABOUT YOUR PARTNER'S FINANCES

1   How much does your partner earn?

2   What insurance does your partner have?

3   What borrowings does your partner have? What are they secured by?

4   Where does your partner want to be financially 10 years from now? 15? 20?

5   What is your partner's approach to money? Is he a spend-thrift? Is she hooked on debt? Does he believe in hoarding money for the future by trimming spending to the absolute minimum now? Is she inclined to think money will 'take care

of itself'? Is he an aggressive investor who wants to actively trade the sharemarket? Is she conservative?

6   Does your partner measure your contribution to the relationship in financial or non-financial terms? If your partner has a strong sense of 'I earn more than you' or 'I'm doing more because I'm paying the bills', control could become an issue.

7   Does your partner gamble or have other addictive habits?

8   Is your partner a financial risk-taker?

9   How honest is your partner about his or her finances?

10 How important is money to your partner? Is it critical to their sense of self-worth or just the means of putting food on the table?

DO I NEED A PRE-NUPTIAL AGREEMENT?

These are more commonly called property-sharing agreements now as the law applies whether you are married or not. Whether or not you are married, your relationship falls under The *Property (Relationships) Act*.

You can draw up an agreement between you that allows you to opt out of the Act but by law the agreement has to meet a number of conditions: it must be written, be signed by both of you, be witnessed by a lawyer and be certified by each party's lawyer declaring that each person has received independent legal advice about the meaning and possible effect of the agreement.

Without such a property-sharing agreement the property will be divided up in accordance with the provisions of the Act. Property-sharing agreements can only be overturned in limited circumstances such as a serious injustice to one partner.

Property-sharing agreements are more commonly used by people who come into a relationship on an unequal footing. For example, you might want an agreement if you own your own home but your partner doesn't. Younger people often tend to be on a relatively equal footing—neither of them owning very much! As time goes on, however, people have more assets. When people have had their assets halved through divorce or the break up of a long-standing relationship they are often quite cautious about the financial risks they are undertaking at the start of a new relationship. It is wise to put financial aspects of your relationship on the agenda as early as possible.

We have tended to assume that only much-married, very wealthy movie stars needed 'pre-nuptials' but there's nothing—except perhaps your sense of romance—to stop you from having one if you feel you need to protect your current financial position.

WHAT'S THE BEST WAY TO SAVE FOR MY OVERSEAS TRIP?

Use a separate bank account and keep your travel finances separate from your everyday spending. As your departure date approaches, scour the travel ads in your newspaper and network through youth hostels so that you can take advantage of any bargains when they come up. Your parents won't thank us for saying this, but many younger people move home for a few months before they leave to help save money faster.

DO I NEED TRAVEL INSURANCE?

Travel insurance covers you for things like lost luggage, medical treatment and losses incurred if, say, your plane is late and you miss your connecting flight from Abu Dhabi. It's medical costs that are the big risk—especially in places like the United States and Japan, where even simple medical treatment can cost an arm and a leg. If you're travelling to these places, it's worth having travel insurance to avoid being financially crippled if you do something dumb, like break a leg. But some countries, such as the United Kingdom, have agreements with the NZ Government so that you can get basic treatment for free. You'll only be in trouble if you can't get into the public system, or you need to be transported back to NZ.

SMART TIP

 If you travel a lot, and are a good credit risk, ask your bank about a gold credit card. Many of these offer free travel insurance if you pay for the trip on the card before you go.

I'M GOING OVERSEAS—WHAT SORT OF MONEY SHOULD I TAKE WITH ME?

All the travel experts say you should take a mix of foreign cash, travellers' cheques and plastic. While you can now withdraw cash from your own bank account using foreign ATMs, anyone who has ever had their card eaten or spat out by one of these machines will tell you there are times when the system doesn't work. Unless you have back-up, that can leave you in a real fix.

Carrying a lot of cash isn't a good idea from a security point of view, but it's a good idea to have some local currency to tide you over when you first arrive. The money change bureaus at airports and railways stations are almost always much more expensive than those in town, but you will need cash to pay for things like getting to your hotel. Travellers' cheques are more secure than cash (if they're lost, they can be replaced), which is probably the main reason people still use them.

CAN I WORK WHILE I'M OVERSEAS?

Kiwis have been working overseas while they're on holidays for years. Often it's the only way to survive on the big OE trip. Most Kiwis who work overseas choose to do so in the United Kingdom, where you can get a two-year working holiday visa if you're under 27. There are other countries that have similar arrangements for Kiwis. You should check with the Ministry of Foreign Affairs and Trade (MFAT) before you leave.

If you're thinking of working overseas, check out the job ads in foreign newspapers (you can often do it online) before you go. Registering with a job agency and networking through youth hostels can also help you find employment.

MOBILE PHONES ARE ESSENTIAL—HOW DO I KEEP THE COSTS UNDER CONTROL?

Mobile phone plans are a bit like bank accounts: there's no such thing as a simple comparison. Money-saving tips from Phonechoice (an Australian site at www.phonechoice.com.au) include:

- Using a landline when you can.
- Carrying a pay phone card and only using your mobile if there's not a pay phone close by.
- Using SMS (text messages) for short messages to other mobiles.
- Clearing the message envelope from your screen so you don't waste a call retrieving old messages. Remember to delete old voice messages as well so you don't have to pay to re-listen to them.
- Check for specials and discounts on your plan and use them. There are often cheap rates offered for calls to other mobiles in the same network.

If budgeting is really a problem, think about using a pre-paid service where you simply pay for your calls in advance and 'top up' your credits when needed.

MY MOBILE PLAN IS TOO EXPENSIVE—CAN I SWITCH TO ANOTHER PROVIDER BEFORE THE END OF MY CONTRACT?

You can, but it may be better to wait until the contract is finished, because you'll usually be hit with a heap of termination charges for leaving early

HOW DO I CHOOSE THE RIGHT PHONE PLAN?

The important thing is to find one that fits your call patterns. Phonechoice say lots of people think they'll only use their mobile for emergencies and sign up for a plan with a low monthly access fee but high call costs. As often as not, they'd be better off using a plan with a slightly higher access fee but lower costs. Take a plan that can be changed. After a few months you can go back to the shop and get advice.

Read the terms and conditions carefully and make sure the network can deliver the coverage you want. You may find that a cheap plan isn't so cheap if you can't use your phone when you need to.

The Consumers Institute has some good reports comparing mobile plans—see www.consumer.org.nz. Again, you'll have to subscribe online for a period if you want to access these but given how much people spend on mobile phone charges it is worth a little expense to choose the right plan.

MONEY ALERT

For many young people, a mobile phone contract is the first complex financial contract they sign. Credit counsellors and lawyers say a common problem is that many don't read the contract and make sure they understand it before they sign. Don't fall into this trap. Make sure you understand exactly what your upfront and ongoing costs are and what it will cost you if you want to get out of the plan.

I BOUGHT A NEW PAIR OF SHOES RECENTLY AND THE STRAP BROKE THE FIRST TIME I WORE THEM—AM I ENTITLED TO A REFUND?

Yes. Shops are required by law to give you a refund if the goods they sold don't do what you were led to believe they would—and you'd probably be entitled to believe you could wear the shoes without them falling apart! Retailers are also required to give you a refund if the goods had a fault that you could not have known about when you bought them, or if they are different from what was described, or a sample you were shown. But they're not obliged to give you a refund if you simply change your mind about an item—even though some retailers do this to keep their customers satisfied.

SMART TIP

Consumer law is comprehensive in NZ. For a quick check on any topic visit www.consumer.org.nz or call them on 0800 CONSUMER. You can get up-to-date information on your rights generally and in specific areas such as cars, credit cards, refunds, lay-bys and door-to-door sales.

I BOUGHT SOME GOODS ON THE INTERNET AND THEY NEVER TURNED UP—WHAT CAN I DO?

If you bought from a NZ company, you have the same legal protections you would have if you had bought goods in a shop. Contact the company first and, if that doesn't work, contact the Consumer Institute. If you bought from an overseas company, your options are more limited, as New Zealand's consumer protection laws don't apply to companies operating in other countries. If you paid using a credit card, ask your bank or card issuer whether you can get a 'chargeback'. Credit card companies will often agree to cancel the payment and reverse the transaction if your goods don't show up.

HOW CAN I PROTECT MYSELF IF I BUY OVER THE INTERNET?

Consumersonline.com.au (the Aussie equivalent of Consumer. org.nz in NZ) suggests these 10 tips:

1 Know who you're dealing with. Make sure you have the company's full name and its full street address. Don't deal with anyone who only gives you a Web address or post office box.

2 Check that the product has a valid guarantee, is legal and will work here.

3 Understand and print out any terms and conditions. Check the due date for delivery.

4 Check the full cost carefully. Watch out for extras such as currency conversion charges, taxes, customs duties, delivery fees and packaging. Who pays for the postage if you have to return the goods?

5 Check the company's online privacy policy. How will your personal details be used?

6 Only use Websites that give you the chance to confirm or reject the order before it's paid for.

7 Print out the order before you send it and keep any reference numbers.

8 Only use secure Websites to pay over the Internet. Don't give away financial information that's not needed to process the purchase.

9 If there's a problem, contact the company asap.

10 Look out for scams—if an offer looks too good to be true, chances are it is.

CHAPTER seven

Protecting your assets—why insurance isn't just for older people

Lots of people think managing money is solely about making your money grow. Not true. An unexpected financial loss can blow your money-making schemes sky high, and it can take years to simply get back to where you started. Insurance isn't the most exciting subject in the world, but a basic understanding of the types of insurance young people may need can help protect you from the unexpected.

I DON'T OWN ANYTHING OF VALUE—WHY SHOULD I CONSIDER INSURANCE?

Let's look at the worst-case scenario. It's the week from hell. You're arguing with your partner while driving the car. You lose control of the vehicle, sideswipe another car and, while trying to avoid hitting a pedestrian, crash into a shop which sells expensive glassware. You get home to find someone has broken into your house and, probably frustrated that you have nothing to steal except for a few CDs, has made off with them and vandalised your furniture for good measure.

What are you going to do? Because you didn't even have third-party property insurance on your car, you're not only minus a car, but the people whose property you damaged in your accident will be looking to you to make good the repairs on their stuff. Your furniture might not have been worth much, but it still needs replacing, and that doesn't come cheap. While it's true that life insurance and serious home contents insurance are more the domain of older people—who have expensive possessions and financial responsibilities—even younger people need to consider basic home contents and car cover. Income protection insurance, which provides you with a regular pay cheque if you're unable to work due to sickness or injury, is another form of insurance that's worth considering.

It's easy to dismiss insurance as a cost that you can't afford. But ask yourself what would happen if something went wrong? If you couldn't afford the consequences, it might be that you're better off making the effort to afford that insurance after all.

HOW DO I 'BUY SMART' SO I HAVE THE INSURANCE COVER I NEED WITHOUT BREAKING MY BUDGET?

There are a few general tips. The first is that most types of insurance policies offer you the option of paying an excess.

This means you pay less for your insurance now, but if something goes wrong and you need to make a claim, you pay the first part of the cost. If you had a $500 excess on your car insurance, for example, and you crashed and needed $2000 worth of repair work, you'd have to pay the first $500 and the insurance company would pay the rest. Excesses can be a great way of bringing the cost of your policy down, especially if you think you're unlikely to make a claim and are prepared to accept the extra costs if you do.

Insurers are also often prepared to offer discounts if you have more than one policy with them. So if you have your car and contents insured with the one company, you should be able to negotiate a lower premium.

Shop around, too, as prices can vary by really silly amounts between insurance companies. Insurance agents and brokers are middle men who can help you find the right insurance policy; however, they won't necessarily have access to all the policies on the market and it's still worth doing a few checks of your own. Ring at least three companies yourself to ask for a quote. The Consumers Institute site (www.consumer. org.nz) has good general tips for every category of insurance. If you want to access their detailed reports, for example, comparing insurance offers from different providers, you will need to join the site. You can do this for an annual fee of $68 or a quarterly fee of $20, which should give you plenty of time to sort out your choice. The information provided on this site may well be useful in negotiating a better deal with your present insurer.

There are also Websites offering online insurance quotes. The NZ Automobile Association Website (www.nzaa.co.nz) offers quotes on home and contents and auto insurance. However, when you're shopping for insurance, make sure you're comparing apples with apples. Cheaper insurance policies often don't provide the same level of cover as the more expensive policies. Shop for the cheapest policy that meets your needs, not just the cheapest one on the market.

CAN I INSURE MY POSSESSIONS IF I'M SHARING A RENTED PROPERTY WITH OTHER PEOPLE?

What insurance companies can baulk at is the situation where one person in the house buys insurance, the house is robbed and they get a huge claim that's clearly hoping to cover everyone else's losses as well. Most policies limit the cover to your own possessions and those owned by family members who live with you, or items for which you are responsible (although policies vary, so check each one closely). If you're in a shared house, you can still get insurance, but it will usually be limited to what you own. It's hard to find a group policy that will cover everyone living there. The odds are that each person in the house will have to get their own individual cover.

MONEY ALERT

 Insurance contracts are probably the most complicated financial documents you're likely to come across, so you need to read them carefully and know exactly what you're covered for. Pay particular attention to any exclusions. These are things that the policy specifically *won't* cover. Often insurance that looks cheap will have a long list of exclusions or, worse still, it will be vague about what is and isn't covered.

WHAT SORT OF CONTENTS INSURANCE DO I NEED? AND HOW MUCH?

The better contents insurance policies give you 'replacement' or 'reinstatement' cover for your possessions. This means that if someone steals your TV, for example, the insurer will pay for a new one of similar size and model. If you want to save money and go down the no frills path, you can buy an indemnity policy, which replaces your goods at their current value. So it would pay less than replacement cost on older items, even though they may have still been in good condition. Other things to check for are whether your possessions are covered if they're taken outside your home, and whether there are any exclusions that would prevent you making a claim.

How much insurance you need to buy is a more difficult question. If you underinsure the value of your possessions, the insurer can argue that you are responsible for part of any losses yourself. You need to sit down and write a list of what you own with realistic replacement values. Some Websites have calculators to help you work out how much you should insure for. Try www.nzaa.co.nz, www.amp.co.nz or www.fintel.co.nz.

WILL THE INSURANCE COVER PRECIOUS ITEMS LIKE MY GRANDMOTHER'S ENGAGEMENT RING?

Insurers will often limit the amount you can claim for things like jewellery and art or similar items (for example, the maximum may be expressed as $1000 for each set or collection, or a higher figure for each claim). If you want cover for more than the minimum, you'll have to list each item and its value separately on the policy. In some cases, you may need to get a formal valuation of the items to show they're worth what you say they are.

MONEY ALERT

Under insurance law you have a 'positive disclosure' obligation. This means you have to notify the insurance company of anything that might increase the risk of your making a claim. If you don't disclose, the insurance company can refuse to pay you when the worst happens and you need to claim on your policy.

AAGH! I JUST GOT A REALLY HIGH QUOTE ON INSURING MY CAR—WHY HAVE INSURANCE COMPANIES GOT IT IN FOR YOUNGER PEOPLE?

The cost of car insurance for younger people is horrendous. It doesn't really help to know that it's because, statistically, younger drivers—and in particular younger male drivers— tend to have more accidents. So you'll usually pay a loading to insure your car if you're under 25.

Many families try to get around this problem by having Mum or Dad insure the car in their name, but if the worst happens, and you have to make a claim, that can backfire. If you were driving the car, and the insurance company didn't know the car was really yours and you were the regular driver, it would be able to argue that you deliberately tried to deceive it when you took out the policy. You didn't fulfil your duty of 'positive disclosure'. To get around this problem, insurance companies often now ask parents to nominate anyone who is a 'regular driver' of the vehicle they're insuring. That puts added pressure on Mum and Dad to let the insurance company know who is really responsible for your car or at the very least, that young people will be driving it.

Younger people also tend to get hit by loadings on the cost of insurance for things like bad driving records and souped-up cars. Indeed, some insurers won't cover cars that have been modified at all. This can include modifications that may seem minor to you, but the insurer feels make your car more susceptible to theft. So you can probably cut the costs of insurance by buying a standard car and sticking to the speed limit!

I SPLURGED ON A SNAZZY NEW CAR—WHAT SORT OF INSURANCE DO I NEED?

If you want to cover your car so that you can replace it if anything happens, you'll need to shop for comprehensive car insurance. This covers damage to your own car as well as damage to other people's property if your car runs amok in an accident. Comprehensive insurance policies allow for your car to be insured either for an agreed value (which will be stated in the policy) or for its current market value. The agreed value is normally better if you want to replace a relatively new car, but check with your insurance company.

Other advice on car insurance from the Motor Trade Association (MTA) is to:

- Watch for generalised or vague terms in the policy document.
- Focus on repair parts, choices of repairer (if any is offered), and the nature of guarantees given.
- Look at the level of the excess and what effect a claim will have on any no-claim bonus you may be eligible for.
- Ask whether there is a dispute resolution system in place.
- See whether there are any extra benefits, such as the provision of a loan car, or reimbursement for rental car expenses if your car is off the road.

MY OLD CLANGER ISN'T WORTH INSURING—DO I NEED TO BOTHER WITH INSURANCE AT ALL?

You should still consider having insurance to cover you if your old clanger damages other people's property. There are two options here. Third-party property insurance covers damage caused by your car to other people's property but not any of the costs of repairing your own car. Third-party fire and theft insurance covers damage caused by your car to other people's property, and also provides limited cover for your car if it is lost or damaged by theft or fire.

It's also a good idea to look for low-cost extensions that are sometimes available with these types of cover. An uninsured motorist extension, for example, can provide limited cover for damage to your car if you were not at fault in an accident and the other driver was not insured.

DON'T I ALREADY HAVE THIRD-PARTY INSURANCE? I THOUGHT IT WAS COMPULSORY.

The third-party insurance that you must take out when you register your car covers anyone who is injured in a car accident. This form of insurance is paid to the ACC (Accident Compensation Corporation) and covers potentially big payouts, such as compensation for someone who is seriously injured by your car. The other third-party policies are not compulsory; they cover damage to property, not people.

MONEY ALERT

Insurance policies usually won't cover damage to your car if you let someone drive it who is drunk or under the influence of drugs, unlicensed, or not authorised under the policy to drive the car. You may also find you're not covered if you drove the car when you knew (or should have known) that it was unroadworthy or unsafe, and this contributed to the accident.

I'VE JUST BOUGHT MY FIRST HOME—WHEN DO I NEED TO INSURE IT?

Immediately. All else aside, most mortgage contracts require you to have your home adequately insured and you could be in default on your home loan if you don't. You can generally get home and contents insurance wrapped up into one package and, like contents insurance, home insurance can vary in what it covers.

There are two main kinds of house insurance: indemnity cover and replacement cover. Indemnity cover will pay out the market value of your house. That, of course, could be far less than it costs to replace your house. Even though this is a cheaper form of insurance it is less frequently used as the homeowner can still be considerably out of pocket and unable to replace the house. Replacement cover, as the name suggests, will pay out the replacement costs. The insurance company will either give you the cash or fund the rebuilding of your home. You get to choose the events you insure against—for example you might have a defined risk policy which insures against loss through fire or you could have a wider policy which insures against virtually all foreseen events. Damage from war, riots and general wear are usually excluded. You need to read your policy carefully—people often think that they have cover when they do not. In some areas companies may refuse to insure against flooding if there is a history of that land being flooded—there have been several such stories reported in NZ media in recent years, most notably in Queenstown which has flooded twice in the last five years.

I'M YOUNG AND HEALTHY—WHY SHOULD I TAKE HEALTH INSURANCE?

Health Insurance allows you to be treated as a private patient if you go into hospital. You can be cared for in a private hospital, or as a private patient in a public hospital, and you can choose your own doctor. Perhaps its most convincing selling point is that it generally allows you to get medical treatment when you need it, rather than having to wait in a queue to be treated in the over-stretched public hospital system. But having said that, there are obvious disadvantages. Health cover is expensive, and many people still end up paying some of the costs of being treated as a private patient. As you're already paying for public health care through taxes, a lot of people feel it's a bit rich to then be paying for private health insurance and part of their health costs as well.

SHOULD I HAVE HOSPITAL ONLY OR COMPREHENSIVE COVER?

There are two main kinds of health insurance: as the name implies, 'hospital cover' covers you for the costs of an operation in a private hospital while 'comprehensive cover' provides for a whole range of medical conditions including doctors' visits. Obviously, the hospital only cover is cheaper. Costs of health insurance vary considerably. Younger people who have good health and are non-smokers pay low premiums compared to older, unhealthy smokers—just what you would expect!

You can reduce the cost of health insurance by agreeing to cover a percentage of the costs yourself, for example, you pay 25 per cent of your bill and the insurance company only has to cover 75 per cent.

Health Insurance costs have risen considerably over the last few years so you need to consider carefully what you really need and for what risks you can afford to cover yourself. Some organisations will cover some health insurance costs for their employees—that is often a very good deal and there may be no sacrifice of salary involved.

If you do choose to take health insurance make sure that you shop around and purchase the best deal for you and your family. Have a look at www.southerncross.co.nz and www.aetna.co.nz to see what the various policies offer and how much they cost.

CHAPTER eight
The big time—buying your own home

Owning your own home has long been the great New Zealand dream. But it's also a big commitment, and one you need to prepare for. Most of us don't, after all, want to end up as slaves to a mortgage, having to work so hard that we don't have the time to enjoy our own little piece of New Zealand. So what do you need to know to find the right balance?

SHOULD I RENT OR BUY?

When your parents were young, the answer was simple: buy. Houses were cheap, and inflation was growing, which meant houses increased in value fast. House prices still have periods where they shoot up but, generally, they have become so expensive that many younger people are questioning the wisdom of saddling themselves with a huge mortgage. Some are saying, 'No thanks' to the mortgage and using their spare cash to invest instead. They reckon they'll do well with their investments and buy a house later on, when they can better afford it.

From a tax viewpoint, there's a lot to be said for owning your own home. This is because any profits you make when you sell are tax free. That may not be true for shares, investment property or other investments. Owning your own home also gives you long-term security—a roof over your head. And while people like to talk about investing in other things, like shares, there's something about regular mortgage payments that forces you to get serious about your finances. It's all too easy to say you'll rent and invest elsewhere, then spend the extra money instead of putting it to work. For many people, having a mortgage is the only way to make sure they'll actually save money instead of frittering it away.

As you can see, there are advantages on both sides; you should be very wary of anyone who tells you there's only one way to go. Chances are that they want to sell you something.

ISN'T RENT DEAD MONEY?

It depends on your viewpoint. Rent is certainly dead money in the sense that it's money going to pay your landlord's mortgage rather than your own. Your landlord, not you, gets the benefits of rising property prices—and the worst bit is that if property prices rise, he'll probably slug you with more rent on the basis that you're living in a more valuable property.

But rent can be worth it if buying a home doesn't suit your financial plans at this stage of your life. What the real estate agents overlook, when they encourage everyone to buy, is that a home and mortgage put a lot of restrictions on your life. If what you really want is the freedom to pick and choose your jobs, to travel, to perhaps try out your skills in a business of your own, acquiring a big mortgage could be the worst thing to do.

Buying and selling property is very expensive. Every time you change you will have costs associated with real estate agents, lawyers, building inspections, bank fees, etc.

There is also a lot of dead money involved in buying a property. It does not make sense to purchase a home if you are likely to have to shift in the next few years.

You have to pay conveyancing costs upfront, and you have to pay mortgage fees for the privilege of getting a loan. There are also ongoing costs, such as rates, insurance and maintenance that you don't have to pay when you're renting.

MONEY ALERT

Are you a renter or buyer? The questions to ask yourself are:

- What's my life looking like for the next five years? Am I ready to make a long-term commitment or do I need to stay flexible?
- How important to me, emotionally, is it to own my own home? Will it make me feel secure?
- How much rent am I paying? What would it cost me to buy the home I want and what would the loan cost me each month? How does rent compare with mortgage repayments?
- Am I prepared to buy a lesser property now and trade up when I can afford it? Or do I want to wait and buy my dream home in one fell swoop?
- How secure is my job? Can I handle a commitment to mortgage repayments?

- If I don't buy, where will I invest my spare cash? What sort of return can I expect?
- Can I afford to maintain my home, pay the rates and other bills if I buy?

I'VE DECIDED TO BUY MY FIRST HOME—HOW MUCH DO I NEED TO SAVE FOR A DEPOSIT?

Some lenders will allow you to borrow up to 95 per cent or more of the value of your home. So if the home you want costs $200 000, you'd need a deposit of $10 000. But here's the catch: to borrow 95 per cent of the value of your home, you will generally need mortgage insurance. This is insurance to protect the lender (not you) if for some reason you can't afford to make your repayments—in which case the lender sells you up, and your house goes for less than the outstanding amount of your loan. You may also need a guarantee from your parents or a very good income.

If your bank demands mortgage insurance, you'll have to pay for it. It costs up to 1 per cent of the value of your loan. To avoid the need for mortgage insurance, you'll generally need to keep your borrowings below 80 to 85 per cent (depending on the lender) of the value of your home. So on a $200 000 property, you'd need a deposit of $30 000.

You'll also need money to cover your legal costs, loan application fees, pest and building inspections as well as rates, moving and having the electricity and phone reconnected. As a rough rule, you need to save up to 2.5 per cent of the purchase price for all these.

HOW MUCH CAN I AFFORD TO BORROW?

Lenders usually don't like you paying more than 25 to 30 per cent of your pre-tax income in loan repayments. Let's say you earn $30000 (around $577 a week). Your lender would probably like you to keep your loan repayments to a maximum of around $750 month. If interest rates were 6 per cent, this means you could borrow up to $116000. But if interest rates were 10 per cent, you could only borrow around $82000.

When interest rates are low, the good lenders also look at your finances to see how you'd cope if rates were to rise. The last thing they want is to sign you up now, and then have to sell your home because you couldn't meet the higher repayments when interest rates rose. During times of low rates, lenders might limit you to a lower percentage of your pre-tax income to give you a bit of padding, if needed. Most lenders now have home loan hotlines where you can get a quick estimate of how much they'll lend you. But be careful—these are estimates, not firm approvals. You should make sure you've got proper approval, in writing, before you buy.

SMART TIP

 If you're borrowing to a buy a home, ask yourself how you'd cope with a 2 or 3 per cent rise in interest rates. If the increased loan repayments make you nervous, don't borrow so much. The banks all have home loan calculators on their Websites where you can play around with different levels of borrowings and interest rates to work out what you can afford.

IS THERE ANYTHING SPECIAL I SHOULD DO WHEN I APPLY FOR A HOME LOAN? WHAT ARE MY CHANCES OF BEING KNOCKED BACK?

To be honest, your chances of being knocked back for a home loan are fairly low. Banks are in business to make money, and they're not going to do that by sitting on all that loot and refusing to lend it out. However, having said that, knockbacks do happen—and not always because you can't afford the loan.

Most lenders now have computerised scoring systems for loan assessments and, if you don't fit into the neat little boxes they've come up with, out you go.

So what are the potential pitfalls? Here are a few of the main ones:

- You've had credit problems in the past.
- You're a part-time or casual worker or your income has been irregular.
- You have changed addresses several times in recent years.
- You are self-employed and your tax returns indicate that you have a low income, or you have only been in business for a short period.

Even if you fall into one or more of these categories, it doesn't mean you can't get a loan. It's just that it may be a bit harder. Talk to lenders before you apply and let them know what the potential problems are. Any half-smart lender will be quick to spot a good prospect who's simply being mucked around by bureaucratic nonsense, and help you out. Try credit unions, PSIS, or solicitors if you cannot get a loan from a bank.

SMART TIP

 Mortgage brokers and consultants can act as your agent in finding the right home loan and are particularly useful for the self-employed and others who fall outside the ideal borrowing requirements. Mortgage brokers generally receive a commission from the lender they match with, though some now offer a fee-for-service arrangement where you pay them for their work rather than their being in the pocket of the lender.

IS IT RISKY BORROWING FROM SMALLER ESTABLISHMENTS? AM I SAFER STICKING WITH THE BIG BANKS?

Who owes who money here? You're going to owe them money, which means most of the risks are on their side. And while service and good systems are important, small lenders can be just as good in this regard as the big players. The major risk, if one exists, is that if your lender gets into trouble—or is sold, for that matter: there will often be a clause in your mortgage contract allowing them to recall your loan. In simple English, that means the lender could ask for their money back and you'd have to find another lender prepared to take over or refinance your loan. When non-bank lenders like Wizard (www.wizard.net) first appeared, the big banks liked to claim they'd be nicer to their customers than the new kids on the block if things turned bad. But with the banks increasingly focusing less on personal relationships with their customers and more on profits, you wouldn't want to pin all your hopes on this.

The best way to reduce your risks, regardless of whether you're dealing with an established bank or a new player, is to take the time to understand your mortgage contract. Okay, it may all seem gobbledygook—despite attempts to explain loan terms more clearly than they used to. But there are some things you really have to know; if you can't understand it from reading the mortgage documents, ask your lender to explain it to you.

Here are the key questions you want answered:

- What happens if I miss a repayment? Are there penalties? If there is a penalty interest rate, how long does it last?
- Under what circumstances can the bank ask me to repay my loan? How long will it give me? (Lots of loan contracts say they must give you 'reasonable notice' if they want their

money back, but don't bother to explain what's reasonable and what's not.)

- Is it possible to restructure my loan if I have difficulty meeting my repayments?
- What are the total fees and charges?
- Does the bank have the right to vary the terms of the mortgage?
- When am I in default on my loan? Believe it or not, some contracts put you in default if you do something like fall behind in your credit card repayments or paint the verandah without telling them first.
- What do they require me to do in addition to making my monthly repayments? Mortgage documents often require you to have the home insured, for starters.

WHY DO THEY HAVE SO MANY DIFFERENT TYPES OF LOANS?

Different loans suit different people. A first home buyer, for example, isn't going to want the same features in a loan as someone with a multi-million dollar home who wants to borrow against it to buy some investments.

Here are the main types of loans and loan add-ons that younger borrowers are likely to come across.

Standard variable loans

Standard variable loans are still the most popular loans on the market. You borrow money, agree to pay it off over 20 or 25 years (it can be more or less), and you make regular repayments, which consist partly of interest and partly of repayment of your borrowings. In the early years, your repayments are mostly paying your interest. But over time, more and more of your repayments will go into eating away at that underlying debt, so that in the final years it disappears fast. The interest rate on standard variable loans fluctuates according to what the money markets and official interest rates are doing. In most cases, your interest rate will rise or fall quickly in response to any announcements by the Reserve Bank on interest rate policy. However, some standard variable loans are structured so that interest rates are reviewed at regular intervals—such as every six or 12 months.

Fixed rate loans

The interest rate on these loans is set when you take the loan out and it doesn't change, no matter what. You can take out a fixed rate loan for a short period, such as one year, or for longer periods. Most fixed loans, however, are for around two or three years. At the end of the loan period, you can 'roll over' into a new fixed rate loan or switch to a variable rate.

The big plus of fixed rate loans is that your repayments stay the same for the fixed rate period. Even if interest rates on other loans double, your rate is locked in. But by the same token, your rate stays the same if rates on other loans fall. You can, in this instance, 'break' the loan and get out early, but you'll be charged a penalty, or 'break costs'—the amount the bank will lose by relending your money at the current interest rate. Fixed rate loans also tend to be less flexible than variable rate loans. You generally can't, for example, have a re-draw facility. But you should be able to find one that allows you to make extra repayments or to pay weekly or fortnightly instead of monthly.

Honeymoon interest rates

Honeymoon interest rates are generally offered as an incentive to take out a standard variable loan. The idea is appealing. You get a low fixed or capped rate (a fixed rate can't go down if rates fall, but a capped rate can) for six months or a year before your loan reverts to the normal home loan rate. If your bank tries to sell you one of these, it will tell you it's to help you cope with the costs of buying your home and moving in. Generous of them. The truth is that they're a marketing gimmick designed to lock you in. They usually come with penalties if you want to get out of the loan early.

SMART TIP

Be sure to compare 'apples with apples'—you need to compare the *total cost* of the loans you are considering. The bank is obliged to tell you the overall finance rate (as opposed to the interest rate quoted) over the period of the loan.

If you are considering a 'honeymoon' offer, be sure to check if there are any penalties or hidden costs at the end of the honeymoon period.

This doesn't mean you shouldn't take advantage of a honeymoon rate if it's offered. But make sure the underlying loan is right for you. Ask the bank what the 'revert rate' is (that's the rate on the normal loan that you'll revert to after the honeymoon period) and compare this rate with that of other loans on offer. If it's still a good deal, that's fine. But it could be that you're better forgetting the honeymoon and just going for a cheap loan.

Lines of credit

Revolving Credit or Lines of Credit allow you to use your home loan like a bank account for your spare cash. You can deposit spare cash into your mortgage, which helps you pay off the loan faster. Instead of having your money in a low-interest bank account and paying tax on any interest you earn, it's reducing the amount you owe on the mortgage— which means you're effectively 'earning' the home loan interest rate tax fee. If you need the money back, you can then re-draw those excess savings. Fees on re-draws can vary significantly, as can the minimum amount you are allowed to take out.

Mortgage offset accounts

Mortgage offset accounts are like revolving credit except for one thing: your savings go into a special 'offset' bank account, rather than going directly into your mortgage account. An offset account is simply a daily banking account linked to your home loan. Instead of earning interest on your deposits, interest on that amount is deducted from your home loan, allowing you to pay off the home loan faster.

The savings you will make will depend on how much money you keep in the account and for how long. But here's a very simple example, showing how it works. Let's say you have a $100 000 25-year home loan at 7 per cent and $10 000 deposited in a mortgage offset account. Assuming you leave the $10 000 in the offset account for the full term of the loan, your total interest bill will be around $75 000, instead of the $112 000 it would be if you had a standard home loan and no offset. You'll pay off the loan in 20 years instead of 25. Of course it's unlikely that you'll leave the $10 000 in the offset account for that long. But even if you only leave it there for the first three years, you'll 'save' around $10 000 in interest on your home loan over its term.

To get the real benefit of an offset account, it should be a 100 per cent offset account—meaning it pays the same interest rate as the lender charges on your home loan. It should also offer a reasonable number of free transactions and give you a choice of home loans that it can be linked to. Most lenders, for example, won't let you link a 100 per cent offset account to a basic home loan, but they will let you link it to the standard variable product.

Flexible repayments

Most borrowers take it for granted that they can make extra repayments to their loan without being penalised and that they have the option of making their repayments weekly or fortnightly instead of monthly. These are all ways of saving big money on your mortgage. But do your checks anyway. Not all loans are this flexible.

SHOULD I FIX MY RATE WHEN INTEREST RATES ARE LOW?

If prices are going to go up, it's common sense to want to lock in a low price. This is what you're doing by taking out a fixed rate mortgage when interest rates are low. But the problem is that people get it wrong. Even economists, who spend years at university studying this stuff, can be downright hopeless when it comes to predicting interest rates. The risk you take is that rates will keep falling instead of rising.

Fixed rates, too, tend to rise and fall much faster than variable interest rates. This is because they move in line with rates on the wholesale money market. So by the time variable rates start rising, and most people start to think of switching to a fixed rate, the fixed rates available have usually leapt ahead of the variable rate increase.

It's better to think of a fixed rate home loan as insurance rather than as a way to make money. It's a guarantee that your interest rate won't rise no matter what happens to interest rates generally. And if you take out that insurance when fixed rates are low, all the better.

MY BANK RECOMMENDS PUTTING MY SALARY INTO THE MORTGAGE, WITH A LINKED CREDIT CARD FOR SPENDING—IS THIS A GOOD IDEA?

The loan you're referring to is an all-in-one mortgage. Instead of having a daily bank account, a home loan and a credit card, you get one account that covers the lot. You arrange to have your pay credited to the account and you can withdraw money from the account as you need it. You also get a linked credit card, which is 'paid' each month by debiting your home loan. This means you're only paying home loan interest rates on your credit card balance, and you're 'earning' home loan interest on your savings (as they're in your loan account).

There are two drawbacks with these loans. First, they may cost more than ordinary home loans. They can have a higher interest rate and sometimes can also carry extra fees and charges. Second, a lot of them are also 'revolving' lines of credit, which means they're not structured to force you to pay off the loan. If you borrow, say, $100 000, and spend up big on your credit card, there's nothing to stop you ending up in 10 years' time still owing that $100 000.

All-in-one mortgages are good for people who are disciplined and great at budgeting, and for more sophisticated borrowers who can justify paying the higher interest rate because they want a revolving line of credit. But if all you want is a cheap home loan to buy your first property, they're probably not value for money. Stick with a loan offering an offset or re-draw facility instead.

HOW DO I FIND THE BEST DEAL FOR ME?

Work out what you want. Do you want a flexible loan with redraw or offset or do you just want a low interest rate? Fixed, variable or split? Do you want to make weekly or fortnightly repayments? Draw up a list of what you want, and shop around. You can get an idea of current interest rates from the personal finance section of the newspapers or from just about any financial Website. A really good place to start your research is www.goodreturns.co.nz. This site compares lending rates from all of the mortgage providers and has lots of other useful information.

I'M THINKING OF BUYING WITH A COUPLE OF FRIENDS—WHAT SORTS OF THINGS SHOULD WE BE LOOKING AT?

Buying with friends can be a fantastic way to get a foot into the housing market without having to live like a refugee. But as anyone who has shared a rental house knows, living with friends can also be a great way to ruin a friendship. So you need to be very careful about who you team up with. Combining with known housemates is a good start—at least you know what they're like to live with. But this is a bigger financial commitment than simply signing a lease, so you need to be sure you want the same things from the house purchase. Remember, all co-owners will be jointly and severally liable for the mortgage payments. That's bankspeak for, 'If your mate doesn't pay his share, we'll chase you for the lot'. So you need to be sure your co-buyers can finance their share of the loan.

It's also smart to get agreement upfront on the big issues such as:

- How will you manage expenses such as rates and repairs to the property?
- How long do you intend to hold the property for?
- What happens if one of you wants to get out early?

It's not a bad idea to draw up a formal agreement on these issues so that there are no arguments later on.

AM I BETTER OFF BUYING AT AUCTION OR PRIVATELY?

The trouble with auctions is that you never know whether you're wasting your time. Anyone who has ever traipsed

MONEY ALERT

If you're buying a house with someone else, you'll need to decide whether you're buying as joint tenants or tenants in common. Any property you own with someone else as joint tenants automatically goes to your co-tenant if you die. If you want to keep control over who it will be left to, buy the property as tenants in common and specify who gets your share in your will.

around the auction viewings knows all too well that real estate agents are great at making you think you can afford the property, and then when you get to the auction, you find it's way out of your price league. If you've already spent money on things like building inspections, that can be enough to turn you off auctions altogether.

But like them or not, more and more properties are being sold at auction, and if it's your dream home that's being auctioned, you don't want to miss out just because you'd prefer to buy at a known price. Here are a few tips to buying at auction:

- If you really want the property, don't be afraid of making a bid before the auction. The seller may be as nervous about the auction as you are and, provided your bid is in the ballpark, may well accept a guaranteed sale now rather than chancing the auction. It doesn't hurt, when you're making the bid, to tell the agent you won't be bidding at the auction.

- Do your research before the auction. Inspect the property several times and ask your lawyer to look over the contract. Once your bid has been successful at an auction, you are required to sign the contract. There's no breathing space for second thoughts.

- Set your limit before the auction and don't go over it.
- Work out a bidding strategy before the auction. Some people like to show 'strength'. They're the ones who bid early and increase the amount of the bid in the hopes of intimidating other bidders and knocking them out. Others prefer to wait until the bidding appears to be petering out before making their move.
- If you suspect you're the only genuine bidder, and the property is below its reserve, stop bidding and negotiate with the agent after the property is passed in. You're only bidding against yourself. If the property is 'on the market', though, chances are the other bidder is genuine.
- If you are too nervous to be sure you'll bid rationally, take someone more experienced along to do it for you.

DO YOU HAVE ANY SMART IDEAS ON HOW I CAN SAVE A HOUSE DEPOSIT FASTER?

Here are five:

1 If they'll have you, consider moving back in with Mum and Dad for six months before you buy your own home. (Hey, if they hate it that much, they may even help you out with the last chunk of savings to get rid of you!) If that's not possible, consider sharing or moving to a cheaper place for the last stretch. You can afford a bit of discomfort in the short term for a place of your own.

2 Hunt down a weekend or part-time job. It doesn't matter what it is because it's not for the long term. The best thing about doing this is that you're not only earning a bit more cash, you're also keeping yourself too busy to spend much.

3 When your deposit goal is within sight, go cold turkey on your spending sprees. Promise yourself a really big

housewarming as a reward once you've moved into your own place.

4 Make sure your savings are invested in a high-interest savings account. Can you get more interest by putting your savings into a term deposit for the last six or 12 months?

5 Do a stocktake on your possessions. Is there anything you don't need anymore that you could sell? Is it worth having a garage sale to make money out of all your junk? You don't want to take unwanted possessions with you when you move into your own place, so why not try to turn them into a bit of extra cash now?

CHAPTER nine
Smart home ownership—how to turn your biggest asset into future wealth

It's one of the unfortunate facts of life that once you've taken the plunge and bought your first home, you'll find the first year tougher than you anticipated. Whether it's unexpected expenses that trip up your plans, an interest rate rise, or just Murphy's law, the odds are you'll find home ownership a huge undertaking. But look on the bright side. You're not paying rent any more and you're investing in an asset that will give you financial security for the rest of your life—if you know how to make the most of it.

HOW CAN I PAY OFF MY HOME LOAN FASTER?

The simple answer is to plough as much money into your mortgage as you can. You can do this in a number of ways:

- Making special one-off repayments when you have a chunk of cash available. This is great for people who get bonuses at work, as you can keep living on your normal income and use the bonus to turbo-charge your loan repayments. If you made a one-off repayment of $1000 at the start of a $150 000 25-year principal and interest mortgage, and interest rates were 6.5 per cent, you'd save around $4000 in interest on your loan and cut the term of the loan by around four months. Make a special repayment of $1000 a year, and the interest bill is reduced by $28 000 and you save around four years off the term of your mortgage.

- Maintaining your repayments at the old level when interest rates fall. Again, let's say you take out a 25-year $150 000 loan at 6.5 per cent. After two years, the interest rate falls to 6 per cent but you keep up your old repayments of $1013 a month. That will save you around $24 000 in interest and cut more than three years off your loan.

- Increasing your repayments each year as your income rises. If you increase your repayment levels by 3 per cent a year, you'll save roughly $47 000 on that 25-year $150 000 loan at 6.5 per cent. And you'll cut more than nine years off your mortgage.

- Making fortnightly or weekly repayments instead of monthly repayments. The monthly repayment on that 25-year $150 000 loan is $1013. If you paid $253 a week instead, you'd save roughly $30 000 in interest and cut more than four years off your loan.

- Using a re-draw facility or offset account. If you could save $100 a month into a re-draw or offset account and leave it there, you would save around $34000 interest and cut almost five years off your 25-year $150000 loan.

You can do all of these calculations yourself on www.consumer.org.nz or www.sorted.org.nz.

HOW FAST, REALISTICALLY, CAN I PAY OFF MY LOAN?

It depends on how much extra cash you have. If you've borrowed $150 000 at 6.5 per cent, your monthly repayments on a 25-year loan will be $1013. If you wanted to pay the loan off in 10 years, you'd need to be putting aside $1703 a month. Five years? Try repayments of $2935.

Five years is probably a bit ambitious, but there's not a huge difference in the repayment levels for longer loan terms. So if you can afford it, it's much cheaper to sign up for a 15 or 20-year loan. If you borrowed $150000 at 6.5 per cent for 20 years, for example, your monthly repayments would be $1118. Even 15 years may be manageable, with monthly repayments of $1307.

I'VE JUST RECEIVED A PAY RISE—SHOULD I USE THE EXTRA MONEY EACH MONTH TO PAY OFF MY HOME LOAN FASTER OR INVEST IT IN SHARES?

The simple rule is that you need to earn an after-tax return higher than the home loan interest rate before you're better off investing than paying off your mortgage. So if your mortgage is costing you 6 per cent, and you're on the 33 per cent personal tax rate, you'd need a return of around 9 per cent before tax to be better off investing.

Financially, you are probably better to pay off the mortgage before investing elsewhere, but many people prefer to establish their investing habit before they have finished paying off their debt.

I'M HAVING TROUBLE WITH MY MORTGAGE REPAYMENTS. WHAT CAN I DO?

Perhaps more than you think. If you're ahead on your loan repayments, and the problem is likely to be temporary, talk to your bank about reducing your repayments for a limited period. Even if you're not ahead with your repayments, if you've been a good customer and can show you're taking steps to solve your financial problems, most lenders will be surprisingly helpful in helping you work through the situation. They may increase the term of the loan so that your repayments are lower or suggest a different repayment schedule that can help you through this hiccup. Re-financing is another option, especially if you have an expensive loan and can benefit from a lower interest rate.

Some people move out when they find their loan repayments are chewing up too much of their income. Some move back in with Mum and Dad for a period; others move into shared accommodation where their rent is much lower than the mortgage repayments. The home owners can then rent out their home and use the rent to help pay the mortgage. Because their home is now an investment property, their mortgage payments are now tax deductible, which helps make them more affordable. If you're in a situation where there's no option but to sell, bite the bullet before your bank acts against you. At least this way you'll keep control of the sale process and can make sure it's sold for the best price possible. Banks are only interested in covering their own debts; not in ensuring that there's something left for you.

MY BANK SAYS IT WILL LEND ME THE MONEY TO BUY A NEW CAR AGAINST THE VALUE OF MY HOME—IS THIS A GOOD IDEA?

It's a great idea for the bank but potentially a horrible one for you. Here's why. I bet your bank told you this was the cheapest way to finance your new car, as you'll only be paying the home loan interest rate. That's true. But did they tell you that unless you're really disciplined about this, you could end up taking as long as 25 years to pay off that car and paying heaps more interest than you would have if you'd taken out a normal car loan? They probably didn't.

MONEY ALERT

Let's say you want to borrow $10000 for a new car. Your options are a car loan for five years with an interest rate of around 8.25 per cent or rolling it into your home loan at 6 per cent. Your home loan still has 20 years to run. If you took the car loan your total interest payments over the next five years would be around $2200, but if you rolled the debt up into your cheaper home loan for the next 20 years, that car loan would cost you around $7000 in interest.

If you want to incorporate purchases for things like cars into your home loan, make sure you structure it so that they're paid off fast. If you paid off the $10000 added to your home loan in five years, instead of 20, the interest cost would fall to around $1600.

SHOULD I TRADE UP TO A BETTER HOME OR BUY AN INVESTMENT PROPERTY?

That's a bit like asking whether you should go out to dinner or buy a new suit for work. It depends entirely on your priorities. You're effectively choosing between a better lifestyle now and investing for your future.

If you're in this position, it's probably a good time to have a hard think about just how much house you need. What sort of home will make you happy and how much are you prepared to sacrifice to get it? It's worth bearing in mind that many financial advisers think most Kiwis are a bit obsessed with having 'too much house'. They keep wanting something bigger and smarter instead of settling for something that suits their needs but doesn't give them a big ego trip.

If you decide you want the better home and an investment property, the question becomes which is the more urgent? If you buy the investment property, realistically, you'll have to put off upgrading to a better home for at least another five years. Can you live with this? But one advantage of buying an investment property is that you're building up a second asset in addition to your home. Unlike your home, which you want to keep to live in, this asset can be sold if there's a profit to be made. And more importantly, it can be rented out. Unlike your home, your investment property can help pay for itself, and the interest on your investment loan should be tax deductible. We'll look at investing in property in more detail in Chapter 13.

HOW CAN I BOOST THE VALUE OF MY HOME WITHOUT SPENDING A FORTUNE?

Don't spend money where it's not needed. It's amazing how many people fiddle about with perfectly good parts of a property instead of concentrating on the problem areas.

Colin and Denise are great at renovating houses. What do they do? Quite simply, they open them up and let the light in. In New Zealand, there is a strong preference for properties that are light, breezy and have a sense of space. So concentrate on the areas that are dark, damp or claustrophobic first. Will a skylight help? What about replacing that cruddy little window with a larger one or some french doors? Can you knock down a non-structural wall to turn two tiny rooms into one larger one at a reasonable cost? If money's tight, even a coat of light-coloured paint and a light carpet (or polished floorboards) can make a room seem bigger and brighter.

Kitchens and bathrooms are another critical area. There's nothing that will turn potential buyers off faster than a dingy bathroom with cracked tiles and peeling paint on the walls, or a grimy kitchen with orange boar's hair carpets and blue walls. You don't have to go the whole hog with granite benches and stainless steel appliances to add value. But it is worth spending a bit of money to make kitchens and bathrooms feel bright, clean and usable.

Don't overlook things like courtyards and gardens, as these can be big 'lifestyle' sellers. Even tidying up the backyard and planting a couple of trees can add value to your home.

But before you go ripping out walls and adding on rooms, there's one word to commit to memory: over-capitalise. You over-capitalise on your home when you spend so much money renovating it that you can no longer sell it for more than it cost you. People tend to sniff at the risks of over-capitalising when property prices are skyrocketing, but it's still one of the most common ways that people lose money on their property transactions. As a rough rule of thumb, valuers say you probably shouldn't spend more than 10 to 20 per cent of the current value of your home on improvements. Of course that doesn't mean you can't do more work later, but wait for your home's value to catch up to what you've invested in it.

MONEY ALERT

Before you undertake any renovations, it's absolutely essential that you fix any structural problems first. We've seen disasters where people have simply painted or plastered over structural problems, only to find that the damp or cracks come back worse than ever after a couple of months. If you have damp problems, get in an expert to advise you on better damp-proofing and ventilation. If walls are cracking, or your floorboards seem springy, you may need to improve the foundations under your home. Get a pest check and, if your property warrants it, a building inspection so that you know exactly what you have to deal with.

HOW MUCH SHOULD I HAVE SAVED FOR EMERGENCY REPAIRS?

It depends on the condition of your home. Experts suggest that it costs about 1 per cent of the home's value each year, just to keep it in the good condition in which you bought it. Obviously, older homes have more potential for things to go wrong than new ones, and repairs don't come up in a nice regular pattern. You may go years without spending much and then be hit with a couple of large bills. This is one more reason to get a building inspection before you buy—you don't want to end up paying large repairs and maintenance bills that you were not expecting!

A sensible plan would be to try to save 1 to 2 per cent of your home's value for emergencies each year. That way if a big expense comes up, you'll at least be partly prepared to pay for it.

I'M THINKING OF SELLING MY HOME. HOW DO I JAZZ IT UP TO GET THE BEST PRICE?

Unless we're talking about a home that could fetch seriously big dollars, you don't want to spend too much preparing for the sale. So here are some tips about changes that are cheap but that will make your home more attractive to potential buyers.

- Make sure your home is clean. Give it a serious spring clean before the inspections start, concentrating on all those areas you normally tend to overlook. Wash your curtains, get the carpets professionally cleaned; if you've got stairs, make sure they're spotless, and make sure the surfaces in the kitchen and bathroom sparkle.
- Get rid of the clutter in your home. You might think it looks lived-in, but buyers aren't interested in your paraphernalia. They want to imagine themselves in the house. Getting rid of all your junk will also make small rooms look bigger. It may even be worthwhile sending some furniture off to stay with friends so that your home looks more spacious.
- Bedrooms are a strong selling point. People have been known to spend a fortune buying lots of crisp white bedding and pillows for property inspections, but you probably don't need to go this far. However, the beds should be freshly made with your best linen. A gentle breeze wafting through an open window is also great.
- Have a friend do a 'sniff' test before you open for inspection. Does your house smell fresh and clean or are there traces of damp, last night's curry, or Moggie's kitty litter hanging around? The old trick of having bread baking in the oven is probably a bit overused by now, but don't overlook the sensory impact of things like a bunch of fresh flowers.
- First impressions are important, so pay particular attention to the approach to your home. If it's a house, is the front yard tidy and appealing? If you live in a unit, are the common areas and lift clean and tidy? I know it's not your job, but if the lift is grubby, it pays to clean it.

- You're selling a lifestyle, not a pile of bricks and mortar. So play to your strengths. If your home has a nice courtyard, make sure it features an appealing set of table and chairs. If the pool is your key drawcard, make sure it's clean and clearly visible. A cold area? Why not set the fire and have the agent light it? Big living room? Then make sure it's arranged so that it looks comfy and inviting. Fantastic barbeque area? Then clean the barbie and have everything set up as though the guests were just arriving.

- Arrange for some 'ambience' music to be playing in the background. Light classical or smooth jazz is fine; heavy metal probably isn't.

- Talk to the agent about the best time for the inspection. If light is a problem, choose the time when the natural light is brightest. If you have a view, when is the best time to show it off?

- Do any minor repairs that need doing. Things like dripping taps and doors coming off their hinges are easy to fix, and if they're not fixed, they give potential buyers the impression that the place is rundown. A quick coat of paint may be needed if you've stuck too many posters on the walls and they're now all marked and blotchy.

- If your home feels sterile or is lacking an outlook, consider investing in some lush new plants to put inside during inspections. These will counteract the problem and you can take them with you when you go!

- Make sure you're happy with the photographs used for advertising your property. Do they create the right impression?

CHAPTER ten

Getting into the driver's seat—
how to make your money work harder

We've always believed there are two stages in smart money management. The first is to make sure you're operating from a sound financial base—that all the little things are in order and you're not going to be hit with an unexpected financial crisis tomorrow. That's what we've been focusing on in the early part of this book. But in the longer term, you don't want to be working to make money—you want your money to be working for you. That's what we're going to look at now.

HOW DO I EARN BETTER RETURNS ON MY SAVINGS?

You start investing. You put your money to work rather than mollycoddling it in a low-interest bank account. The key thing to understand about investing is that it's all about risk and reward. Instead of leaving your money safe in a bank account, you take a risk with it. And if that risk pays off, you'll get a much better return.

But that's not to say investing is like gambling—even though lots of people buy shares thinking it is. Smart investing is about taking calculated risks that increase the likelihood of the reward.

WHEN CAN I START INVESTING?

There's no real time limit on when you can invest, though it is important to invest with money that you can afford to commit for the long term. It's tempting to think you'll invest your house deposit savings in the sharemarket in the hope of reaching your goal sooner, but if the market falls, you'll find you either have to sell at a loss or put off your home purchase until it recovers.

When you're starting out, it's probably best to use money that you can afford to lose. I'm not saying you will lose it. In fact, much of the next few chapters will concentrate on ways to make sure you don't lose your investment. But you need freedom to take risks and you won't have that freedom if you're scared of suffering a loss.

HOW MUCH DO I NEED BEFORE I CAN START INVESTING?

A start of $1000 is fine; $5000 is even better. But if you're really itching to get going, there are ways you can start investing with $1. There's no minimum on share investments, but brokerage—the money you pay to buy and sell your shares—is a bit prohibitive if you're dealing with small amounts. If you trade on the Internet, you can generally buy or sell shares for around $20. That's a cost of only 1 per cent if you're buying a $2000 share parcel, but it's 10 per cent if you're only investing $200. So you'd probably want to keep your share purchases above at least $1000.

Of course investing doesn't just have to be in funds or shares. You can keep your money in a high-interest bank account or in a bonus saver account which rewards you with a higher interest rate if you add to your investment each month. One of the arguments for building up your money in an account like this is that you can start your share or fund investments with a bigger lump sum, and that gives you a greater choice.

SHOULD I TAKE OUT A LOAN TO START MY INVESTMENT PORTFOLIO?

Borrowing to invest is a time-honoured Kiwi tradition. There are two main attractions to going down this route: getting leverage and tax-deductible interest.

The first attraction is that you have more money to put to work for you. In investment parlance this is called 'leverage'. Let's say you have $1000. If you invest it for five years, and earn 10 per cent each year, you'll end up with $1610 before tax (assuming you reinvest all your income). But if you borrow another $4000 so that you've got $5000 to invest, you'll end up with $8053. That's a profit of more than $3000, rather than $600.

The key to leveraging your investments is that the return you get must exceed the interest rate you pay on the loan. If the interest rate here was 7 per cent (and, for simplicity, let's assume you use a loan where you only have to pay the interest in advance each year; you repay the principal in full at the end of the five years), you'll pay out $1400 over the five years in interest. After you've paid your interest, and repaid the loan, you'll be left with $2172 from your investment. That's still much better than only investing your own $1000.

But think what would have happened if your investment had returned only 5 per cent. If you'd invested your own $1000, you'd have $1276 after five years. It's not much of a result, but you've still made money. But if you'd borrowed $4000 at 7 per cent, you'd end up with just $757 after you repaid your loan. You'd have lost some of your original $1000. And if your investment return had been negative, you could have lost your entire $1,000 stake and more.

The second attraction of leverage is that the interest you pay on investment loans is generally tax deductible. (The loan has to be for an income-producing investment for the interest to be tax deductible. So you could run into problems, for instance, if you borrow to invest in a vacant block of land.) So the tax man helps fund your investment. Taxation is investment friendly—not only can you claim the interest costs of your borrowing for investment purposes but you also get to keep the gains you make. New Zealand, in contrast to many other countries, has no Capital Gains Tax (CGT). That means that you get to keep the capital growth that your investment (may) make—the rise in the value of your investment property; the growth in the value of your shares, etc. When you sell the property or the shares you are not taxed on that gain.

The big danger of borrowing to invest, especially when you're just starting out, is that it increases your risks. If the investment turns out to be a dud, you still have to pay your interest and repay the loan. As we just saw in the example above, you could end up losing money instead of making it. You also have to find the cash to meet your interest payments each year while your investment is growing.

In 1999 in Australia, lots of people found out the hard way that borrowing to invest can be painful if things go wrong. When the Australian Government offered the second round shares in Telstra, everyone wanted them. The first Telstra share offer had done really well, so people borrowed money through all sorts of means—even on their credit cards—to buy the second lot of shares, thinking they were a sure thing. Telstra's share price got a real hammering over the next year and these investors found themselves committed to a loan that was worth much more than their shares.

It comes down to your level of confidence and your ability to repay the loan. Unless you rate fairly high on both counts, you might be better waiting to borrow until you have a bit more experience.

SMART TIP

I know one financial planner who reckons a small loan can be a great way to get started. He believes most of us are much more disciplined when it comes to paying off a loan than we are about saving. He suggests borrowing small to start with and using all your spare cash to pay off the loan as quickly as possible. You may only borrow $5000, as it's important that the debt is manageable. The problem with borrowing is that most people think in big numbers, not smaller, easier-to-manage ones. The good thing about this strategy is that if you can pay off the debt quickly, you soon have an unencumbered investment earning money for you. Then, if you desire, you can borrow again for another investment. You gradually build up a larger loan and portfolio rather than taking big risks upfront.

WHERE DO I START? I DON'T EVEN UNDERSTAND WHAT HALF THESE THINGS ARE!

Why don't we run through the basics of what your investment options are? All investments can be broken down in two ways. The first is what type of investment they are, and the second is how they're structured. There are four main types of investments, which the professionals tend to refer to as 'asset classes':

Cash

Yep, this is as simple as the folding stuff in your wallet. Or, more accurately, the money in your bank account. The distinguishing features of cash investments are that they earn interest and you can withdraw them at any time—they're not locked away. In investment parlance, 'cash' investments generally include interest-earning investments that are locked away for less than a year. So a six-month cash deposit would be considered cash. As a general rule, the risks of investing in cash are low, but you won't earn much on your money either. Over the long term, cash investments usually don't earn much more than the inflation rate.

Fixed interest investments

Think of a term deposit. It also has two distinguishing features: your money is locked away for a fixed period; and the term deposit pays a fixed rate of interest that is locked in at the outset. All fixed interest investments have these two qualities and typically they lock your money in for a year or more. But unlike term deposits, most fixed-interest investments can be traded: if you don't want to hold them for the full term, you can sell them to someone else.

With fixed interest investments, you're generally promised your money back when the term of the investment is over. So they're also regarded as 'safe' investments. But during the term, interest rates can rise and fall and that affects the daily value of your investment. If you have an investment earning 5 per cent, and interest rates rise to 6 per cent, obviously no one is going to want to buy your investment from you, unless you offer it at a cut price. But if rates fell to 4 per cent, you'd have a long line of people ready to buy your investment, which is returning 5 per cent. You could increase the price and still find a buyer.

Because of this risk, fixed interest investments tend to provide higher returns than cash—though you can also lose money on them if you sell them before the end of the term.

Property

Property is probably the easiest asset class to understand because we're all familiar with it. But what are its investment qualities? For starters, property has something in common with both cash and fixed interest investments: it can provide you with an income. But instead of earning interest on your investment, the income from property comes from rent.

While you're not locked into a property investment for a fixed term, it's not like cash either. It generally takes at least six weeks to sell a property (and often a lot longer), so it's not a great investment for people who need to keep their money accessible. In investment talk, this is an 'illiquid' investment.

There's also another big difference between property and cash investments. Let's say you need $1000. Do you sell your home to get the money or take it out of the bank? Of course you take it out of the bank. It would be sheer idiocy to sell a house worth hundreds of thousands of dollars just because you need $1000. So property is a 'lumpy' investment: you need big licks of money to buy it and you can't sell off part of it if you need some cash. Ever heard of anyone selling their bathroom to buy a new car?

On the positive side, property can, as we all know, deliver big profits through price increases. It's not like cash, or even fixed-interest investments, where you invest and someone promises to give you your money back. But history has shown that property tends to increase in value over time. This makes it a 'growth' investment. You buy property hoping to sell it for a higher price, but you accept the risk that prices may fall. Over the long term, most investors are rewarded for the extra risks they take by returns that are higher than those from cash or fixed interest investments.

Equity

The best known equity investment is shares. Equity investments are simply investments that give you a stake in a business and a share in its profits. Imagine a business—we'll call it Telecom. If one person owned this business, they'd have to be a squillionaire, as it's worth around $9 billion. But Telecom has been broken up into 1.9 billion shares, each of which can be bought and sold separately, and each of which entitles the owner to one 1.9-billionth of the overall business. So even a small investor can have ownership or 'equity' in Telecom.

Like the other investment classes, equity investments can give you an income. Many companies share part of their profits with investors each year, through payments known as dividends. But unlike cash or fixed interest investments, there's no guarantee you'll get a dividend, so the income from equity investments can be a bit iffy.

Because shares are bought and sold daily, and because companies are broken up into so many tiny shares, it's relatively easy to get your money out of an equity investment.

Unlike property, if you need $1000, you can put part of your share portfolio on the market and in most cases it can be sold within minutes.

But, like property, equity investments are growth investments. They can rise in value and they can fall. In fact, one consequence of them being traded so often is that they can rise and fall in value much more quickly than property, which can sometimes make shares seem more like a rollercoaster ride than an investment. But over the long term the risks are rewarded. Shares can provide returns higher than other investments.

Various types of financial products have been developed to allow you to invest in these major asset classes. Here are the main ones you're likely to come across.

Cash

In addition to that bank account, cash investments include bank bills and cash management trusts. Bank bills are mainly for larger investors. They are a way for investors to lend money to banks for a short period—often 30 or 90 days. You generally need at least $10 000 and preferably $50 000 or more to buy bank bills, but people do buy them, because they pay better interest rates than normal bank accounts.

Cash management trusts are professionally managed investment products that give small investors access to bank bills and other cash investments. You can invest in a cash management trust with as little as $1000; you will pay a fee to the fund manager—about 1 per cent a year—to look after your money.

Fixed interest

While most ordinary investors are familiar with term deposits, the most common fixed interest investments are often known as bonds. Bonds are used by governments, banks and companies to borrow money at a fixed rate for a fixed length of time. They're a bit like fixed rate home loans for the big end of town. These borrowers want to lock in their interest rate so they don't have to worry about future interest rate movements. The most common bonds are those that last for two, three, five and 10 years.

For small investors, there are bond funds (also known as fixed interest funds) where professional fund managers invest your money for you.

Property

When most of us think of property investments, we think of a holiday home or a rental unit. But that's only part of the picture. Many people invest in so-called commercial property investments—hotels, offices, factories and shops. There are also managed investment funds for property investors. Some are traded on the Stock Exchange just like shares; these are called listed property trusts. Others can be bought direct from the fund management company. To make matters even more confusing, there are managed funds that invest in listed property trusts; these are called property securities funds.

Equity

As before, the most common form of equity investment is shares. There are also share funds that you can invest in with even small amounts of money; with these you let a professional fund manager do all the work for you. You can invest in shares in overseas companies as well as New Zealand companies.

HOW DO I DECIDE WHICH ASSETS ARE RIGHT FOR ME?

It's time for a bit of self-analysis. You need to think about your financial objectives and the trade-offs you're prepared to make between risk and reward. Try these questions to get you started.

- What sort of return do I want from my investments?
- How much of my money am I prepared to lose to chase that return?
- Do I need income from my investments or am I looking for growth? Do I want a mix of the two? If so, which is the more important?
- How long am I prepared to invest for?
- Do I want a consistent investment or am I prepared to accept something that's up one minute and down the next?
- Am I prone to panic? What would I do if I woke up one morning to find my investment had halved in value?

If you want to have a bit of fun, there are now investment risk profilers on the Internet. There's a money personality quiz at www.sorted.org.nz and also a risk profiler. There is also a good risk profile to be found on the Australian site www.financialpassages.com.au. They'll give you an idea of how much risk you can tolerate—and the investments best suited to that risk level. Ultimately, the decision is up to you.

As a general rule, the investments producing the higher levels of income, such as cash and fixed interest, provide investors with a smoother ride—fewer risks but lower returns. Growth investments such as shares and property should provide higher returns over time, but they can be volatile and you should commit to your investment for the longer term. Three years would be the bare minimum; five to seven years is better. That way you can take advantage of the potential for long-term growth and ignore daily fluctuations.

SMART TIP

Younger investors have a real advantage when it comes to investing, as they've plenty of time to ride out market falls and watch this money grow. They can have more of this money in growth investments than, say, someone nearing retirement, who knows that in a couple of years they won't be working anymore and their investments will have to provide them with money to live on.

IF I WANT HIGH RETURNS, DO I PUT ALL MY MONEY IN SHARES?

An all-share portfolio won't suit everyone, and there have been periods when shares have done worse than other asset classes—and for a long time. Financial planners generally recommend that investors have a mix of asset classes in their portfolio. You'll hear them banging on all the time about diversification and not putting all your eggs in one basket. But it makes sense.

The table on the following page shows how the different asset classes have performed each year from 1981 to 2001. The figures in italics indicate which asset class did best each year. As you can see, the numbers are all over the place, and as often as not the best performing asset class in one year turned out to be a real dog the next year.

Unfortunately, unsophisticated investors (and many more sophisticated investors who should know better) invest their money in the investments that have been showing the highest returns. They reckon that if the return is so high, the investment must be good. But often they buy in at exactly the wrong time, when the investment or asset class has become overpriced and vulnerable. Instead of making money, they lose it. In reality, investors would often be better to invest in the asset class that had done worst over the past year than in the one with the highest returns. This is called counter-cyclical investing.

ASSET CLASS RETURNS

Date	New Zealand				International	
	Cash	Bonds	Property	Shares	Bonds	Shares
2002	5.76	8.68	*19.02*	4.2	-18.89	-36.68
2001	5.98	4.79	12.12	*16.71*	-1.25	-16.74
2000	6.68	11.08	7.34	-9.09	*19.75*	2.65
1999	4.91	0.06	-6.39	16.98	-8.11	*.23*
1998	7.75	14.09	4.8	-3.3	26.59	*37.78*
1997	7.9	6.79	6.61	2.91	21.73	*41.24*
1996	9.75	8.8	*23.32*	18.66	-4.17	5.43
1995	9.42	13.22	13.87	*19.61*	17.09	19.33
1994	*6.64*	-2.79	2.79	-6.89	-8.16	-8.18
1993	6.7	13.52	-5.56	*51.71*	5.8	13.71
1992	6.99	11.82	-39.23	*13.41*	12.76	0.41
1991	10.78	20.57	-11.37	*30.67*	28.27	29.8
1990	*14.86*	14.39	-58.14	-35.93	11.93	-15.5
1989	14.42	15.88	-20.74	18.13	12.13	*23.95*
1988	16.66	17.69	-21.37	-6.75	10.46	*-29.31*
1987	23.86	*23.94*	-70.7	-48.55	-7.89	-6.89
1986	20.54	16.77			20.41	*35.98*
1985	26.49					35.66
1984	15.82					45.13
1983	14.33					37.97
1982	18.34					25.73
1981	16.22					12.87

2001 Returns

	Cash	Bonds	Property	Shares	Bonds	Shares
3 year	5.85	5.22	4.05	*7.47*	2.81	1.68
5 year	6.64	7.25	4.71	3.32	10.86	*15.39*
7 year	7.47	8.32	8.48	8.35	9.43	*14.46*
10 year	7.26	7.99	0.42	*10.88*	6.82	10.38

2002 Returns

	Cash	Bonds	Property	Shares	Bonds	Shares
3 year	6.14	8.15	*12.73*	3.4	-1.38	-18.51
5 year	6.21	*7.63*	7.04	4.58	2.21	-1.72
7 year	6.95	7.67	*9.16*	6.24	3.84	4.55
10 year	7.14	7.68	7.4	*9.94*	3.51	5.41

Note: *Italics* indicate best performers.

(*Source:* Morningstar)

When you diversify your investments, you spread your risk. If one investment or asset class does badly, your other investments should make up some of the shortfall. You're also guaranteed of getting a slice of the best performance in each period.

I'M CONFUSED ABOUT WHAT PEOPLE MEAN BY DIVERSIFICATION. DOES IT MEAN I NEED EQUAL AMOUNTS IN CASH, FIXED INTEREST, PROPERTY AND SHARES?

Some investment portfolios used to be based on a 30/30/30/10 principle. That means they'd have 30 per cent of their money in shares, in fixed interest and in property, and 10 per cent in cash. But while that's probably great from a diversification point of view, it's a lousy idea. It assumes that everyone has the same investment needs and objectives and, as we've just seen, that's not true.

Diversification is about starting with a split like this and modifying it until it gives you the result you want. A younger, more aggressive investor, for instance, could easily have more money in shares and property. Some advisers would say younger people can afford to have almost all their money in property and shares. This is because time is on the side of the younger investor. You will, however, want to have some cash available for emergencies—a good rule of thumb is to have 2–3 months' cash available. It can take time to release your money out of property or share investments—and you don't want to have to sell them at a time when prices are not favourable to you. The very act of selling them costs you as well—and that can be quite a lot in a property sale.

Diversification also means having a mix of investments within each asset class. One of our favourite stories here came from Rob Prugue, who works in the Australian finance industry.

Rob had been to one of the money shows they have in major cities, at a time when tech shares were all the rage. One investor came up to him and said: 'It's a no-brainer. I sold my international share fund, which had returned a measly 12 per cent, and put the money in a tech fund which had delivered 60 per cent.'

Rob was horrified: 'What about diversification?'

'No worries. This fund is diversified across Australian and international tech shares.'

Many who invested heavily in technology shares felt that they were well—diversified—after all, they had shares in many different kinds of technology businesses in different countries. However, as they no doubt found out when the tech bubble burst in 2000, they weren't diversified at all. In a share portfolio, being diversified means having shares in companies from a *range* of industries—banking, mining, retail, manufacturing, media and so on. Having shares in overseas companies as well as New Zealand ones only helps the diversification if the companies are in different businesses.

In the fixed interest market, diversification is about the term and quality of your investments. You want some short-term investments and some that are long term. You can get a higher return from investments with a lower credit rating (for example, bonds issued by a company versus bonds issued by the Government), but you wouldn't want all your fixed interest money in bonds offered by companies with low credit ratings.

Diversification gets a bit harder when it comes to property investments. Not many of us can afford to go out and buy a range of properties in different cities or set ourselves up with a residential property investment, a hotel, a shop, an office and a factory. But often property funds can give you this type of spread.

HOW CAN I DIVERSIFY IF I ONLY HAVE A SMALL AMOUNT TO INVEST? IF I DIVERSIFIED MY MONEY I'D END UP WITH ABOUT $10 IN EACH INVESTMENT!

Financial advisers generally suggest you start off in a managed fund. These are investment products that are managed by professional investment managers. Instead of going it alone, you put your money into a fund where it is pooled with the savings of a lot of other investors. The fund manager then goes out and buys a whole heap of investments which you own part of.

There are two reasons financial advisers like managed funds. The first is that fund managers generally pay them a commission for putting people into funds. Not all financial advisers take these commissions—we'll talk about how to choose a financial adviser in Chapter 11. But for now, let's just say they have a vested interest.

The second reason is that managed funds give you access to a range of investments rather than putting all your eggs in one basket. So instead of buying shares in just one company—which could go broke tomorrow—your $1000 can get you into a fund that invests in a wide range of different companies. You get instant diversification.

Lots of first-timers start off in what's called a balanced fund. These give you a bit of all the main asset classes— shares, fixed interest, cash and property—as well as a mix of investments in each. So you have one investment, but within that you probably get $10 worth of everything. The big advantage of balanced funds is that you can diversify with just a small amount of money and leave the problem of doing your own diversification until you've built up enough investment dollars to make the exercise worthwhile. But you'll still need to ensure that you choose a balanced fund that has similar investment objectives to your own. Some balanced funds have only a small amount of their money in shares; others can have as much as 80 or even 90 per cent.

MONEY ALERT

Unfortunately, there's no easy way to get rich quick. Young investors should steer well clear of anything that promises incredibly high returns for low risk and little work. Other warning signs for scams are:

- Lots of exclamation marks and capital letters in the ads.
- No 'real life' address—just an email address, or PO box.
- Lots of assurances that the scheme is legal.

DON'T SMART INVESTORS GET IN BEFORE PRICES RISE AND SELL OUT AT THE TOP?

If you could buy low and sell at the top, you could hire yourself out and run your own investment fund. The fact is that markets can move quickly and unexpectedly. What looks obvious with the benefit of hindsight probably wasn't that obvious to investors at the time.

Take the tech share bubble we were talking about earlier. It was obvious to many investors from as early as 1998 that technology shares were selling for more than they were worth. All through 1999, smart investors were saying that the market was overheating and would crash. They were right . . .

But the crash didn't come until April 2000 and, in the meantime, the returns earned by the doomsayers (who were not investing in tech shares) were minuscule compared with the returns of investors riding the tech bubble. They could predict *which way* the market would go, but they couldn't predict exactly *when* it would happen.

As those investors in 1999 also found, it can be hard to stick to your guns when the markets appear to be moving against you. If the market's going up, and you think it's going to crash, you feel smug and superior for a time. But if the market keeps rising you start to doubt your judgement. Everyone else is making big money and you're not. Fear and greed come into play. You start to fear that you're missing out on a once-in-a-lifetime opportunity to cash in quick. Finally, greed takes over. You buy against your better judgement and find you were right all along: the market crashes just as you predicted.

If you believe the market will rise, but it keeps falling, the same emotions come into play. At first you feel smarter than the average investor. While they're selling, you're in there buying, convinced that you're getting a bargain. But as the market keeps falling you start to doubt your judgement. Maybe this time things won't recover. You get frightened and panic. And if you're like most investors, you'll find you panicked and sold right at the bottom of the market.

Time in the market is more important than timing.

According to figures from BT Funds Management, one of the biggest risks investors face is being out of investment markets at the wrong time, rather than being in them at the wrong time. How do they figure that? BT looked at the returns on the Australian sharemarket between 31 December 1989 and 31 December 1999. If you'd been in the market for every one of these days, you'd have earned a shade over 10 per cent a year. But if you'd missed just 10 days—and they happened to be the 10 best days for the sharemarket—that return fell to under 6 per cent a year. If you missed just a month—the 30 best trading days—you'd have lost money. That's a huge risk to take.

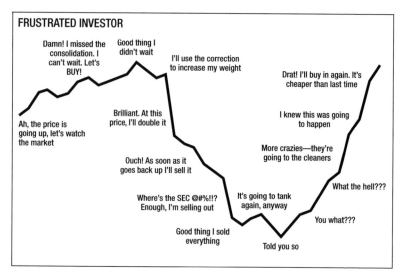

(*Source:* BTFM)

BT also looked at the case of two investors who put $5000 a year into the Australian sharemarket every year between 1979 and 2000. Annie invested at the best possible time each year; Bill invested at the worst possible time. How do you reckon they fared? If you said Annie did better than Bill, you're right. But if you said Bill bombed out on his investments, the results might surprise you. While Annie ended up with just under $607 000 from her investment efforts, Bill came out with almost $441 000. Both had invested $100 000 and both had earned several times that in investment returns. It was being in the market that was important; being lucky enough to pick the best days to buy was just a bonus.

SMART TIP

Not investing all your money at once means that you can take advantage of a strategy known as dollar cost averaging. By making a commitment to invest a set amount each month (or at another interval if monthly investments don't suit), you're investing regardless of what the markets are doing. When prices are low, you get more shares or fund units or whatever than you do when prices are high, so you benefit when prices recover.

Let's say you decide to invest $100 a month in a managed fund. In the first month, the unit price is $1, so you get 100 units. In the second month, the price has fallen to 50 cents; your $100 buys you 200 units. (Don't worry—most managed funds are much less volatile than this one.) In month three, the unit price has soared back to $1.50. You buy 66 units.

You have invested $300 to buy 366 units in the fund. With each unit worth $1.50, your investment is now worth $549—an average return of 83 per cent.

CHAPTER eleven
No-hands investing—
let someone do the hard work for you

Let's face it. Not everyone wants to do a lot of hard work choosing and monitoring investments. While there are some people who get a kick out of this stuff, others just want to get on with their lives in the knowledge their money is growing. That's why one of the fastest-growing industries in the world is managing other people's money. So what do you need to know to become a good 'investment delegator'?

WHERE DO I FIND A MANAGED FUND?

Managed funds have traditionally been distributed by financial advisers and planners. They put together an investment plan to suit you and recommend investment products. We'll come back to financial planners—and how to pick a good one—in a minute.

Many younger investors who are just starting out feel they don't have the money or don't need to see an expert about their finances. They'd prefer to invest directly themselves and think about getting expert advice later, when they've got a few investments already in hand.

If you go it alone, a good place to start is on the Websites of discount brokers. As well as letting you trade in shares, most also offer access to managed funds where you can invest without paying the hefty fees that you often get slugged with if you go to a fund manager yourself or invest through a financial planner who is paid a commission. (That's because the 'fee' goes into the adviser's pocket as commission.) Discount brokers such as Access (www.accessbrokerage.co.nz) let you choose your investments online for a flat fee of $29.50. Research groups such as Morningstar and Fundsource track the performance of managed funds and you can access this info online for free. These groups analyse the funds and give ratings—a bit like the star system for hotels. They're not infallible—and different groups can disagree on how highly a fund manager should be rated—but they're a start.

Don't forget to keep in mind your investment objectives and risk profile, as discussed in Chapter 10. Even if you're starting off with a balanced fund that invests in all the main asset classes, there's no point in going for an aggressive balanced fund with most of its money in shares if you're the sort of person who can't sleep at night because you're worried about making a loss. Similarly, if your objective is to grow your money fast, and you don't mind a bit of risk, you don't want to be stuck in a conservative balanced fund that's aiming to produce a consistent, but unexciting, return.

SMART TIP

Kick off your managed fund research by looking at www.fundsource.co.nz.

I HAVE A SHORTLIST OF FUNDS—WHAT HAPPENS NEXT?

Managed funds in New Zealand must be sold through an offer document (called a prospectus) that has been approved by the New Zealand Securities Commission (www.sec-com.govt.nz).

Prospectuses can be horrible documents. That's why research shows a lot of investors don't bother to read them. But a good prospectus should tell you what you need to know to make an investment decision without giving you a headache or an inferiority complex. If a prospectus is incomprehensible, look for another fund: if the fund manager can't communicate what it's doing with investors' money, it doesn't deserve your business.

The questions you want the prospectus to answer include:

- Where will my money be invested?
- What sorts of returns can I expect in the short term and over the longer term?
- What are the chances of losing money in any 12-month period?
- What risks are involved in this investment? (Be very wary if the fund manager appears to gloss over the risks.)
- What's the recommended timeframe for this investment?

- Who will be managing my money? How experienced are they?
- What are the costs and how will they impact on my investment?
- How do I get my money back?
- Where do I complain if I'm not happy?
- If the investment is offering tax breaks, does it have a 'product ruling' or 'binding ruling' confirming these from the IRD?

If you are happy with the prospectus and decide to invest, you fill out the form and buy a number of units in the fund. Each unit entitles you to a share of the income distributed each year from the fund; if the value of the fund's investments rises, the value of your units will increase proportionately.

You can keep track of the unit price through the managed fund tables published each week in most major metropolitan daily newspapers and also in the *Sunday Star Times*. Your fund manager should also send you a quarterly report on the progress of the fund.

If you're investing online, you'll also get a copy of the prospectus. To invest, you'll generally have to download the prospectus and send off the application form by snail mail, though in some cases you can now fill out the form and invest online.

SMART TIP

If you don't need the income from your fund, why not ask for it to be reinvested? That way the money will be used to buy more units and you'll build up the value of your investment. But remember, as far as the tax office is concerned, you'll have received the income and you'll have to pay tax on it. So you'll need to keep some cash aside for this.

I HAVE GOT $1000 TO INVEST—HOW DO I ACCELERATE MY INVESTMENT PLAN?

Once you've made your first investment, the key is to get the essential D ingredient into your wealth plan. The D is for DISCIPLINE. You can pat yourself on the back for having taken that important first step, but unless you're prepared to keep adding to your investment, that $1000, even if it earns 10 per cent, will barely move. You'll go nowhere fast.

The good news is that the fund managers have made discipline dead easy. When you make your first investment, you'll see a section on the application form referring to the fund's savings plan. If you sign up for this, a fixed amount will be automatically taken out of your bank account each month and used to buy more units in the fund. Some savings plans allow you to set aside as little as $50 or $100 a month—that's just $25 a week. But if you sign up for $100 a month, that's $1200 a year that's automatically being invested for you. After five years, you'll have invested almost $6000—and that's before you add on your investment earnings. Savings plans are also a great way to use the strategy we looked at in Chapter 10—dollar cost averaging—where you're adding to your investment through good markets and bad.

HOW LONG SHOULD I BUILD MY FIRST INVESTMENT FOR BEFORE I CONSIDER A SECOND INVESTMENT?

There are no firm rules on this one. It depends on a range of factors, such as whether you're satisfied with your original investment; whether your investment objectives have changed; whether you've come across attractive new investment opportunities; and how many investments you want to keep track of. While you want to end up with a diversified portfolio, the fact is that you're not going to get there overnight. When we asked financial planner Laura Menschik, of Millennium Financial Services, about this, she said you need to build up a reasonable amount before it becomes practical to spread your money across several funds or a mix of direct investments and funds. Having small investments all over the place can be a real pain in the backside. You'd be much safer, for example, having at least $5000 in a balanced fund, but you might want to think of diversifying if that $5000 was all invested in a single company's shares.

I CAN'T MAKE HEAD NOR TAIL OF MY MANAGED FUND STATEMENT— WHAT ON EARTH DO ALL THE FIGURES MEAN?

Most managed funds operate through a legal structure known as a unit trust. You don't have to worry too much about the technicalities of this, except to understand that these trusts are required by law to distribute all the income they receive each year to investors. (If they don't, they'll have to pay tax, and the idea of a managed fund is that you pay the tax yourself.)

In order to fill out your tax return correctly, the fund has to break down all your income into the relevant tax categories. If the fund receives dividends on share investments, and these dividends carry special tax credits known as imputation credits, these will be itemised separately. Property trusts often provide tax breaks on their income because of other types of tax allowances, so these will also be listed separately.

The income distributed from the fund may also include things like the profits the fund manager made by selling investments. These are known as 'realised capital gains' and are also listed separately on your statement. (The profits on investments that are still held by the fund are known as un-realised capital gains, as the fund hasn't sold them. They do, however, increase the value of your units in the fund.)

WHAT WILL A MANAGED FUND COST ME?

The costs of individual funds should be clearly spelt out in the prospectus—ideally, showing both the fees as a percentage of your investment and the dollars involved. As a general rule, the more complex the fund, the higher the fees. You'd expect to pay less for a cash fund than for a fund that invests in shares, for instance.

The types of fees can vary, but let's take a look at the main ones.

Entry fees

These range from zero to around 5 per cent of your invest-ment. Generally, cash funds have no entry fee and NZ and overseas share funds have an entry fee of 4 or 5 per cent. Almost all the entry fee goes to financial planners as commis-sion for selling the fund. If you bypass the planner and go directly to the fund manager, you'll still have to pay it, because the fund managers don't want to upset the planners. Incestuous, isn't it?

The good news is that discount brokers and advisers who charge a fee for their service will give you back most of the entry fee. You can usually arrange for this money to be 'rebated' to you in the form of extra units in the fund so that all your money is invested.

Management fees

The fund manager charges an annual fee for investing your money. This is usually a percentage of the value of the fund and it's taken out before you get your returns. Like entry fees, ongoing fees vary according to the type of investment. But you're looking at around 0.5 to 1 per cent for cash funds, and around 1.5 to 2 per cent for share funds.

Expenses

In addition to the manager's fee, investors also have to pay for the costs of running the fund—things like auditor's fees and the costs of printing a prospectus. Some expenses are paid by the fund manager, but others aren't. In addition to the management fees, the prospectus should tell you the Management Expense Ratio of the fund. This is an overall figure that includes the management fee as well as these other costs, making it a much better indicator of the ongoing cost of the fund. Again, the numbers vary, but think in terms of around 1 per cent for a cash fund and 2 per cent for a share fund.

MONEY ALERT

Investors often don't realise that financial planners are paid an ongoing 'trail' commission for each year you remain with the fund. That's paid on top of any commission they get for selling you the investment. If you're being charged a fee for ongoing advice, ask them to refund you this trail commission. They don't need to be paid twice.

Exit fees

Sometimes a fund manager will not charge an entry fee. Instead the fund will charge an exit fee if you cash in or redeem your investment within a certain period. Exit fees usually operate on a sliding scale—the longer you stay with the fund, the lower the exit fee. A fund may, for example, charge 3 per cent if you exit within the first year but only 2 per cent if you leave after three years and zero if you stay with the fund for five years or more.

Performance fees

These are more common with specialist funds—such as venture capital or hedge funds. (Confused? A venture capital fund invests in companies that are just starting up. A hedge fund tries to make money out of falling markets as well as rising ones.) The fund manager usually takes a share of the investment return if it exceeds a set rate each year.

The buy/sell spread

Theoretically, when you invest in, say, a share fund, the fund manager has to take your money and buy shares on your behalf. When you sell, the fund has to sell your shares so that you get your cash back.

Many funds charge these transaction costs back to investors so that they are not borne by people who stay in the fund. The charges are reflected in different prices for buying and selling units in the fund.

CAN I CALCULATE THE OVERALL RETURN ON MY MANAGED FUND? WITH ALL THESE FEES AND DIFFERENT SORTS OF INCOME, I'M NOT SURE WHETHER THE FUND IS PERFORMING WELL OR NOT

This can be confusing. The managed fund tables on the Internet and in newspapers give returns over periods such as one or two years, but they may not include things like the upfront fee you paid to get into the fund. And because they are calculated over a fixed period, such as one year, they don't necessarily show what your experience has been.

But it's not that hard to do the numbers yourself. How much did you originally invest? If you want to look at your total return (including the impact of those entry fees), this is the figure you start with. If you want to look at the actual return from the fund, after the fee was paid, simply use your starting balance with the fund. If you invested $1000, but paid a 4 per cent entry fee, for example, your starting balance would be $960.

How much income have you received from the fund? (Don't include any income you've reinvested; this will be accounted for in the value of your units.) Add the income to your starting balance. So if you invested $1000 and received income of $50, you now have a figure of $1050.

Now look at the current exit price for the fund. We use the exit price because this is what you'd get if you sold your units today.

Multiply the exit price by the number of units you own. If you've taken your income, you should have the same number of units that you originally bought. But if you've reinvested your income, you'll have bought more units—it's the new total number of units that you should use.

Let's say you bought 1000 units at $1 each, took your income, and the unit price is now $1.05. Your $1000 has grown to $1050. Add the income to the value of your investment, and you've got a current investment value of $1100—a 10 per cent return. You don't need to worry about things like the annual management fee—these are deducted from the fund before you calculate your return. But you do have to include exit fees if you want to know what your net return would be if you sold tomorrow.

Let's say your fund has a 2 per cent exit fee. Two per cent of $1050 is $22, so you'd leave the fund with $1028 plus the $50 income you've already got—a total of $1078. Your net return over the term of the investment is 7.8 per cent. Note that if you'd reinvested your income, the exit fee would be calculated on a higher amount, as all your earnings would still be in the fund. That's a good reason to avoid funds with exit fees.

A FRIEND TOLD ME HE HAS HIS MONEY IN BIO-TECH AND HEDGE FUNDS. THAT SOUNDS A LOT MORE EXCITING THAN MY BORING OLD SHARE FUND. SHOULD I PUT MY MONEY THERE INSTEAD?

Once you get to start looking at managed funds you'll be amazed at how many different ones there are on the market. Some of the other exotic ones include funds focusing on resource shares, technology shares, big brand names, south east Asia, and 'geared' share funds that borrow to buy shares. They're all marketed on the basis that they're giving you access to an area of investing that's likely to provide higher returns over the long run. But before you get too excited, consider this: in 1999 there was a rush of technology funds onto the market, all promising to do better than the average share fund. They were brought out at the height of the tech frenzy and investors rushed them—at the worst possible time. When the tech bubble burst, these funds lost big-time, because they'd invested the money at the top of the market. Too often fund managers see the launch of new funds as a marketing opportunity, rather than trying to do the right thing by their investors. In this case, many didn't even bother to tell their investors that they already had exposure to tech companies through their 'boring old share funds'.

Financial planners use these specialist funds to add spice to their clients' portfolios. If an investor has a diversified portfolio and wants some money in hedge funds or bio-tech, they might shift a small proportion of the money that way. But you'd be putting all your eggs in one basket if all you had was a bio-tech fund.

I'M LOOKING FOR A SHARE FUND—SHOULD I USE ONE THAT INVESTS IN NEW ZEALAND OR OVERSEAS SHARES?

If you put all the sharemarkets in the world together, New Zealand would make up less than 1 per cent of the total. So you're not really very diversified at all if all your money is invested in New Zealand. You'll also find that many of the world's best performing companies are not New Zealand—Microsoft, Nokia, Coca-Cola and Johnson & Johnson, for example. Some entire industries that may be very good investments are unrepresented on the New Zealand sharemarket—pharmaceuticals, mining, oil exploration, etc. You miss a lot of opportunities if you don't look outside our own market.

On the other hand, New Zealand shares offer some advantages that overseas shares don't—tax credits on dividends, for starters.

Financial analysts have found that adding overseas shares to your portfolio can actually increase your longer-term returns while at the same time reducing your risks. That's diversification at work again. So the answer to the question is: have both.

I DISLIKE COMPANIES THAT DESTROY THE ENVIRONMENT OR EXPLOIT THIRD WORLD LABOUR—ARE THERE ANY FUNDS THAT STEER CLEAR OF THESE COMPANIES?

Yes, there are. They're called ethical funds, and they've been a big growth market over recent years. Their performance hasn't been bad either. It seems doing good and making money can be compatible, after all. The definition of what's ethical and what's not varies from fund to fund. Some focus more on the environment; others on social issues. Some have a blanket ban on investments in companies operating in businesses that they are opposed to. The older style of ethical investment, for example, black-listed investments in things like uranium mining, cigarettes, gambling, arms and alcohol. Others try to identify companies in businesses that will improve the environment or society. They might look at companies in sustainable agriculture, waste treatment or bio-technology, or companies that create youth employment. There is a good Australian website concerned with socially responsible investing at www.ethicalinvestor.com.au.

I THINK I NEED SOME ADVICE. HOW DO I FIND A GOOD FINANCIAL PLANNER?

Word of mouth is still the best recommendation. Presumably you want someone who is accessible to where you live or work, so talk to friends and other people in the area and make a note if a particular name keeps cropping up. Go where the smart money is—if you have friends who are doing really well with their personal finances and investments ask them for a referral to good advisors. Advisers in NZ do not have to be licensed so you should take care whom you use. The Financial Planners and Insurers Association (FPIA) can give you a list of advisers in your area. The FPIA website is at www.fpia.org.nz. There are also lists of planners by geographical area on www.goodreturns.co.nz. Ideally, you need to come up with a shortlist of two or three possible advisers who can meet your needs. Advisers who are members of the FPIA are also subject to its rules.

If you're happy with all that, it's time to make an introductory appointment. Check upfront that the adviser can handle your business—and that they're not only interested in people with big sums of money to invest. Most advisers will agree to an initial 'get-to-know-you' meeting without charge, but don't expect them to solve all your problems at this meeting. What you're trying to do is to get a feel for the adviser; to see whether they understand where you're coming from and can genuinely help, as opposed to just giving you a sales pitch.

But do give the adviser the courtesy of planning for the meeting. Gather together details of your income, debts and savings capacity. Think carefully about your financial goals—both short and longer term—and have a clear idea of what you want to know.

Advisers won't make specific recommendations at this stage. Instead, they will outline what they can do for you. The adviser shouldn't try to push you into anything at this stage, so run for the hills if they're into the hard sell or suggest products or strategies that don't seem to fit your needs.

CHAPTER twelve

A share of the action—how to make money on the sharemarket

If you decide to invest on your own, chances are that sooner or later you'll buy some shares. Investing in shares can be a great way to make money, but if you don't know what you're doing, it can also be a great way to lose it. So what do you need to know?

AM I BETTER OFF INVESTING IN SHARES NOW AND BUYING A HOUSE LATER?

As we discussed in Chapter 7, there are arguments both ways. A lot of younger people are taking their time and learning to invest before taking on the burden of a mortgage, but regardless of how old you are, or what your priorities are, Kiwis are increasingly coming to accept that it makes sound sense to have part of their money invested in the sharemarket.

In the past, shares were a bit mysterious for the ordinary person. They were some sort of strange thing traded by men in suits; they didn't have much relevance to the rest of us. But shares are just a way of giving you part-ownership of companies. Companies are split up into millions of little parts and you can buy and sell each part on a market known as the Stock Exchange.

By buying shares, you can invest in the companies that are part of daily life—whether you want shares in something high profile, such as Coca-Cola or Kiwibank, or in a company like Resmed, which is leading the world in treating sleep disorders. As a part-owner of these companies, you share in their profits—both through income that they pay out to shareholders (known as dividends) and through any increases in the value of the company as it grows its business (known as capital growth).

BUT AREN'T SHARES TERRIBLY RISKY?

It's true that share prices jump around a lot. Indeed, if your only experience of the sharemarket is listening to the reports each night on the news, you'd have good reason to think share prices swing up and down with frightening regularity and often for no reason at all. But over the longer term, the sharemarket tends to be much more rational. If companies are growing their businesses and profits, their share prices will rise (sooner or later). But if the company is experiencing problems, the share price will fall.

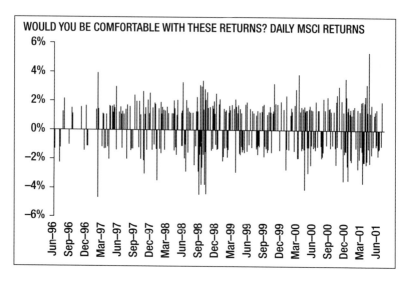

(*Source:* Credit Suisse Asset Management)

Here's another way of looking at the risk involved in share investments. The graph above, showing daily MSCI (Morgan Stanley Capital Index) returns, indicates the price movements of an international index of shares for each day over the five years to June 2001. As you can see, there are big changes from day to day and no real rhyme or reason as to why they occur.

But if you spread out all those returns so that they only show what happened over each three months during this period, you can see the swings weren't so bad at all—this is the second graph.

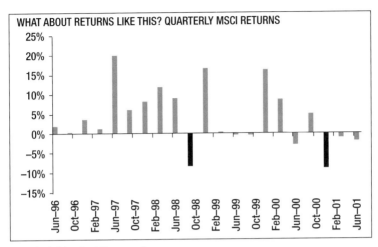

(*Source:* Credit Suisse Asset Management)

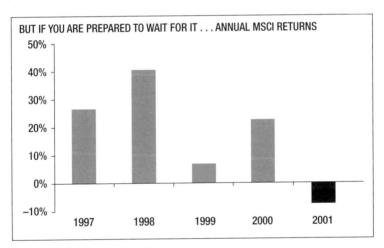

(*Source:* Credit Suisse Asset Management)

And if you measured the performance of the shares over each year, you'd have only lost money in one year—2001: this is the final graph. (Though, we have to say, the last two years were somewhat dismal as well.)

So what do these graphs tell you? The obvious conclusion is that shares can be extremely risky if you're investing on a day-to-day basis. But if you're prepared to commit to the longer term, you miss a lot of the day-to-day volatility. You can also reduce the risks of investing in shares by remembering the basic principle of diversifying your investments. If you hold a spread of shares in different companies, you then run less risk of losing all of your dosh if one company runs into problems.

WHAT SORT OF RETURNS CAN I EXPECT FROM THE SHAREMARKET?

We've all heard the stories of people who have increased their money tenfold in a matter of weeks by investing on the sharemarket, right? Wrong. These people may have struck it lucky with a share that turned into a skyrocket. And just as you can make your fortune, or lose your shirt, by gambling at the racetrack, you can do exactly the same thing on the sharemarket.

Over the long term, a portfolio of quality shares should give you a return of around 6 to 8 per cent above the inflation rate. So if inflation was 3 per cent, for example, you might earn 9 to 11 per cent from shares. But those figures hide a range of shorter-term returns. Throughout the twentieth century there were several crashes where share prices fell by more than 50 per cent. And several years when share prices rose by 40 or 50 per cent.

It's worth remembering that share investments also offer tax advantages. The dividend imputation system (see page 161) gives you tax breaks on the dividends you receive. You also get to keep any capital gain in the value of your shares if your intention at the time of purchase was investing rather than trading.

HOW DO I GET STARTED?

Your first step is to find a broker. You can't buy or sell shares without one. Even if you don't plan to start investing immediately, you'll need to have a broking account up and running before you kick off. The New Zealand Stock Exchange (NZX) is a good place to start looking for a broker. The Website at www.nzx.com has a list of broker firms and members of the stock exchange. The *Yellow Pages* will also have listings of stockbrokers in your area. You can choose between a full service broker, who will send you research and help with advice on which shares to buy, or a discount broker, who will simply perform your trades for you. Most discount brokers operate over the phone or the Internet. While they don't offer personal advice, many online brokers have research on different companies on their Websites and may even have buy and sell recommendations.

In some cases, brokers will require you to open a special broking account and deposit cash with them. The broker will then take money out of this account when you buy shares, and put money in when you sell them. If that doesn't appeal, most brokers also allow you to set up a direct debit facility so they can transfer money in and out of your bank account to cover your share transactions.

SMART TIP

Websites such as www.goodreturns.co.nz can help you search for a broker. As always, ask around—friends and family members who have some experience in investing may be able to direct you to someone who will be a suitable match for your needs.

I HAVE CASH, I HAVE A BROKER, AND I'M READY TO ROLL. WHAT'S NEXT?

The next step is the most exciting one—working out what you want to buy. Unless you have a lot of savings, or have just landed a fat inheritance from long-lost Aunt Bertha, you're not going to be able to diversify straight away. So you need to think about your longer-term goal before you get started. What sort of share portfolio do you want to build up over the next few years?

It's really tempting when you decide to start investing to rush in and buy the first shares you think of, just so you can feel you've got started. But there's no rush, and it's better to take the time to make a plan than to dash off in the wrong direction.

Think back to your financial needs and objectives. What do you want from your shares? Are they part of your long-term wealth creation plan or just an outlet for your 'play money'? Are you looking for high growth? Or do you want a more stable portfolio that gives you an income? How much risk are you prepared to take? If you're worried about losing money, it is better to concentrate on solid companies paying good and sustainable dividends than to chase the latest hot stock. More aggressive investors can afford to add a bit more risk to their portfolios.

How much time can you spend choosing and monitoring your share portfolio? I think it's a myth to talk about shares that you can buy and forget about, but there's no doubt that more conservative investments, such as the big quality companies, require less day-to-day monitoring than more risky investments.

Thinking about these sorts of issues will give you a better idea of where you want to start. Read the finance pages of your newspaper to find out what's happening in the business world. What sort of companies are doing well? Which ones are in trouble? What are the men in suits saying about the prospects for our economy?

Have a look at the sharemarket indices published in

your newspaper. There are the main indices, such as the NZSX 50, which tracks the broad performance of shares on the New Zealand market, but there are lots of sector (or industry) indices too. There are also indices based on particular industries such as tourism and leisure, technology, forestry, etc., which track how they are performing on the market. Remember that you are buying a share in a business. So think about which companies should be doing well and which ones you'd expect to be struggling.

It might be worth running a dummy portfolio for a month or longer. Pretend to invest in companies that take your interest. Keep a record of your purchase price and see how you go. One of the most common problems experienced by new investors is not realising how fast the sharemarket reacts to good or bad news. You turn on the news after you get home from work: Telecom has just announced a new billion-dollar deal that's predicted to grow its profits by 20 per cent over the next two years. 'Yes, please,' you think. 'I'd like a share in that.' You buy Telecom shares the following day, not realising they've already risen by a huge amount and you're buying in at a record price.

A few days later, the share price starts to fall as the share analysts look at the deal and start to assess the risks involved. You feel you've been cheated. You sell. You've fallen into the other trap for inexperienced investors: not realising that the sharemarket often overreacts to both good and bad news in the short term, leading to wild swings in share prices. But as heads cool, and things settle down, the shares go back to trading at more sustainable values.

If you run a dummy portfolio, you may find that you are reacting to the latest news or rumour instead of taking a longer-term view. Better to do that with pretend money than with your own real money.

SMART TIP

At the time of writing the NZ Stock Exchange was revamping its Website—now at www.nzx.com. It promises forthcoming information on the fundamentals of investing.

I'VE TRIED LOOKING AT THE SHARE PRICES IN MY NEWSPAPER—WHAT DO ALL THE FIGURES MEAN?

The information comes straight from the Stock Exchange; you'll find similar information if you check share prices online or use an online broker. Here are the main items you'll come across.

The share code

This is simply a three-letter shorthand code for the name of each company. When you buy shares, your broker will lodge an order for CEN for example, rather than spelling out the name Contact Energy. Similarly, if you want to check a company's share price online, you'll need to enter the code. If you're unsure of a company's code, most online brokers and the NZX Website have search facilities where you can find them. There are good Websites where you can track what is happening with particular shares—try www.stockwatch.co.nz or www.sharechat.co.nz.

Where there is more than one type of share for the company, the extra shares will be given additional letters to separate them from the ordinary shares. Fletcher Forests (FFS) for example, has a class of shares that have different voting rights from its other shares. The code for these shares is FFSPA (Fletcher Forests Preference Shares).

52 week high and low

This is the highest and lowest price that the shares in the company closed trading at over the past 12 months.

Last sale

This is the price at which the share closed at the end of the day's trading, if you're reading the newspaper. If you're looking at 'live' prices on the Internet, it is literally the price the shares last traded at. (Note, though, that some Websites report share prices after a 20-minute delay, and the price may well have moved in the meantime. They do this because they pay a cheaper royalty to the Stock Exchange for delayed prices than for live prices.)

Volume or numbers sold

This is the number of shares that were traded on the day if you're looking at end-of-day prices such as those quoted in the newspapers. If you're looking at live data, you can see the number of shares traded so far today. Obviously bigger companies have more shares traded; some small companies may go for days without seeing their shares traded at all. Shares with a high level of trading are known as 'liquid', because you can buy or sell without any trouble. 'Illiquid' shares are more risky because you may not be able to find a buyer if you want to get out.

Day's range of sales or prices

The highest and lowest prices the share traded at during the day.

Buy and sell quotes

When you buy shares, your broker puts in a bid on your behalf. You may, for example, put in an order to buy Sky City at $8.30.

This is listed along with the bids of everyone else who wants to buy Sky City shares on the Stock Exchange's automated trading system. Sellers also put in bids. When a 'buy' bid and a 'sell' or 'ask' bid match up, the shares are traded.

If you're looking at quotes on the Internet, what you'll see are the highest bid to buy the shares and the lowest bid to sell them. You'll also be able to see how many shares are on offer at this price. In the newspaper, you'll see the bids that were standing when the market closed the previous day.

Dividend

The dividend column simply shows the level of the previous year's dividend in cents. Usually, there will be some indication in the legend whether the dividends are carrying imputation credits.

Dividend yield

This is the dividend as a proportion of the share price. So a share worth $1 paying a 5c dividend will have a 5 per cent dividend yield.

PE ratio

This is a common statistic used by investors to judge whether or not a share is expensive. It is the company's share price divided by its earnings per share. A PE of 20 means a company's share price is 20 times its earnings; a PE of 10 means the share price is only 10 times earnings.

SMART TIP

If you're trading over the Internet, you should also be able to look at market depth. This shows the 10 highest buy bids and the 10 lowest sell bids for the shares, along with how many buyers or sellers are recorded at each level and how many shares they want to buy or sell. Market depth figures are a good indicator of the strength of the market. If there are a lot of buyers near the current price, chances are you'll have to bid around the current price to get your shares. But if buyers are thin on the ground, then you may be able to bid lower and still get the shares that you're after.

WHAT'S AN IMPUTED DIVIDEND?

As we discussed earlier, dividends are simply part of the company's profits that is paid out to shareholders. In many cases, the company has paid tax on those profits already, but dividends are also taxed as part of your income. If there wasn't some sort of system in place to deal with this, dividends would end up being taxed twice—in the company as profits, and in your hands as income.

Under the dividend imputation system, companies can attach tax or 'imputation' credits to dividends to reflect the tax that the company has paid. An imputed dividend is simply a dividend that carries these credits. You may get a fully imputed dividend, which means it carries tax credits at the full company tax rate of 33 per cent. Or the dividend may be only partly imputed, which means the tax paid by the company was less than 33 per cent. You'll also come across references to unimputed dividends, which don't carry any tax credits.

When you fill out your tax return, you must declare the full amount of the dividend, including the imputation credit. So if you got, for example, a $1 dividend, with 25 cents of imputation credits, you'd have to declare the full $1.25 in your income. However, once you've calculated the tax on your dividend, you can then use the imputation credit to reduce your tax bill.

HOW DOES DIVIDEND IMPUTATION WORK?

You receive a fully imputed dividend of $1 and declare $1.50 as income in your tax return. If you're on the 33 per cent tax rate, you'll owe 50 cents tax on the dividend. But you then claim the 50c tax credit, and your tax bill is cancelled out. If you are on a lower tax rate, you can use the unused credits to offset tax on other income; but if you're on a higher tax rate, you'll have to pay a bit more tax on your dividend.

I'VE FOUND HEAPS OF SHARE TIPS IN ONLINE CHAT ROOMS—HOW DO I KNOW WHETHER THEY'RE ANY GOOD?

You don't—and that's the problem. Chat rooms are simply sites where people with a common interest can get together to swap notes. It's a bit like talking over drinks at the pub—except that with chat rooms you can't see who you're talking to. The good thing about chat rooms is that you can learn from other investors' experiences. But before you start investing on the basis of what you've read there, have a look at the disclaimer on the site. It's sobering stuff. The chat room operator certainly isn't taking responsibility for any dud tips you get there, so the risk is all yours.

You may also have read about crackdowns on people who were 'ramping' shares over the Internet in recent years. Ramping shares isn't anything new; it's been happening for donkey's years. But the Internet has made it easier to do because news travels faster.

How does it work? Typically, someone looking to ramp shares gets themselves set by buying shares in a small company. (It's much easier to ramp shares in smaller companies, where there are not a lot of shares on issue, than in big companies, where there are millions of shares issued. This is because you need to buy fewer shares to have an impact on the share price.) They then start spreading the 'news' through chat sites and other forums, saying they have some inside information and the shares are about to take off. Often, they're in league with someone else who then logs on and confirms they've heard the same rumours. They might even buy a few more shares at inflated prices to whet the appetites of mug investors. But long before the buying frenzy finishes (and people realise the good news isn't for real), the original per-petrators sell their shares at a profit. In Australia a few years back, a 17-year-old student was on a popular Website posing as Coles Myer's managing director. He posted a notice about the company's upcoming profit results in an attempt to boost the share price. Fortunately, someone at Coles spotted the notice and referred it to the regulators.

Share ramping is illegal in New Zealand (and in most overseas markets) and the regulators are constantly on the lookout for it. The better chat room operators are also keen to crack down on this sort of misuse of their Websites. But if the old saying, 'Don't believe everything you read in the papers', is true, you should be even more careful not to believe every-thing you read on Websites.

I'VE HEARD THAT SMALLER COMPANIES PROVIDE BETTER RETURNS THAN BLUE CHIPS. IS THIS TRUE?

The best investments are companies that grow their profits year in, year out. These may be small companies that will one day be big companies; or they may be big companies that just keep getting better. The advantage of investing in smaller companies is that they generally have lower share prices than bigger companies, and so can provide bigger profits from small price movements. Let's say Company A has a share price of $10 and Company B has a share price of $1. Shares in both companies rise by 20 cents. For investors in Company A, that's a small return on their money—only 2 per cent. But investors in Company B have a 20 per cent return on their $1 investment. By the same token, while a 20c fall is just a minor blip for an investor in a big company, it can be seriously bad news for an investor in a small company.

If you build up a diversified portfolio, you'll ideally have some of your money in smaller companies and some in the larger blue chips. You may want to consider a small companies fund for your small company investment. There are several good funds on the market that concentrate on sorting through the thousands of small companies on the sharemarket and picking the better ones. This also ensures that you get a diversified exposure to small companies—and don't put all your eggs in a basket that goes broke.

MONEY ALERT

Don't make the mistake of thinking that a company's shares are cheap because you don't have to pay a lot for them. It's the relationship between the company's share price and the company's earnings that determines whether the share is cheap or expensive. A company with a $20 share price but a PE ratio of 10, for instance, should be better value than a company with a 20 cent share price that is making a loss or has a high PE ratio.

HOW DO I CHOOSE WHICH COMPANIES TO INVEST IN?

As I've said before, when you buy shares you're buying part of a business. So it's that business you really need to look at. You don't have to be an accountant or financial whiz to do this. Once you've worked out your financial needs and goals, you should be able to come up with a shortlist of companies that might suit your interests. Then grab a copy of their latest annual report, or log onto their Website, and find out a bit more about what they do and how they're faring. Some questions you might like to ask are:

- Does the company specialise in one area or does it have a number of different businesses? If it specialises, and is good at what it does, this can make it hard for other companies to compete with it. But on the downside, it may also be vulnerable to any downturns in its industry. A company with several businesses may be better placed to withstand a downturn, but the risks there are that it may lack direction.

- Is the company in a growth industry or one which is mature or declining? Industries such as health care and finance have been tipped as industries likely to grow as our population ages.

- How strong are the company's competitors? The best investments tend to be companies that have strong positions in their industries and can dictate the terms on which they do business. But companies in very competitive industries are forced to keep prices lower, and may also find that they're competing for the supplies they need.

- How easy is it for new competitors to come into the market and take some of the company's business? What alternative products or services is the company competing with? Newspapers, for example, are a business where it's very difficult for new competitors to break into the market. You need to invest a lot of money in equipment and people to put out a newspaper, and there are few people around with pockets that deep. But newspapers are also competing with other sources of information—both traditional competitors (TV) and newer technologies (the Internet).

- How vulnerable is the company to changes in the economy? Some industries, such as food, chug away no matter what the economy is doing—we all have to eat. But others, such as building product manufacturers, tend to be more influenced by economic conditions. If the economy slows down, building activity also slows down. (Companies whose profits are heavily dependent on the economy are referred to as 'cyclical' companies.)
- Does the company pay imputed dividends? What is its dividend yield? Does it have a good history of growing its dividends? Is dividend growth likely to continue into the future?
- What is the company's PE ratio and, more importantly, its prospective PE ratio (based on estimated future earnings)?
- How good is the company's management? Is the management team relatively stable? Do they have a clear strategy for where the company is going?

If it sounds a bit daunting, don't be put off. The only way to learn about investing is to try, and to accept that you will make mistakes. Have a look at the companies on your short-list, and think about their businesses. Then look at how much the shares are selling for and invest in those you feel comfortable will do better than the average and are selling at a reasonable price. Lots of people start by investing in companies they know from their everyday dealings. You don't need to be a financial genius to work out whether your bank, phone company or supermarket is in the business of winning customers or losing them! Try to reduce your risks by spreading your investment across different types of stocks (maybe a food and a building materials company if you are unsure of whether the economy will slow down or keep growing) and sticking with companies with quality earnings.

HOW DO I KNOW WHEN IT'S A GOOD TIME TO BUY? ARE THERE ANY SIGNALS I SHOULD WATCH FOR?

We all want to buy at the bottom of the market and sell at the top. And there are few things more satisfying than buying shares when you think they're cheap and watching them rise. However, as we discussed in Chapter 9, timing the market is a lot easier in retrospect than it is in reality. And if you have a long-term approach, it doesn't matter all that much when you buy and sell, so long as you are buying good investments.

But obviously it makes sense to buy shares in companies that are good value and look likely to grow their earnings and to sell shares in companies that are overpriced or likely to run into problems. So what are some of the signs that will tell us if the company's likely to be a good buy, or a bad one?

Signs that a company may be undervalued include:

- It is trading on a low PE ratio compared with similar companies or the PE ratio it has traditionally traded at. (This may also be a sign that it has problems in its business or poor growth prospects.)
- It has a high dividend yield. (See previous comment.)
- Every time you pick up the newspaper or turn on the news, someone is criticising the company. Often a good investment is countercyclical—running in the opposite direction of 'fashion'. (But be careful: this could also be a sign that the company is in strife.)
- The industry which the company is in is unfashionable at the moment. (Investors tend to move in cycles. One minute they're all in love with banking shares; the next week it's media or mining.)
- Directors are buying the company's shares. (Annual reports carry details of directors' dealings, showing which directors have bought and sold shares in their own companies. This

can be an illuminating piece of information for investors.)

- The company is being touted as a potential takeover target. (This is particularly true when the NZ$ is weak and it is cheap for overseas companies to buy New Zealand businesses.)

- There has been some bad news recently that has sent share prices tumbling—even though the company is still making profits. An example here was the sell-off of shares following the September 11 attacks in the US in 2001.

- The company has announced some temporary bad news— such as a lower profit forecast—which has sent its share price tumbling further than is warranted. (You often see big share price falls when a company announces a small drop in profit, even though profits are likely to bounce back again in the future. But if the bad news is long term, the shares are likely to keep falling.)

Signs that a company may be overvalued include:

- It has a high PE ratio compared with similar companies or the PE ratio it has traditionally traded at.

- It has a low dividend yield (though some companies, like Guinness Peat Group (GPG), have always had low dividend yields because they reinvest their profits rather than paying them out to shareholders).

- The company is flavour of the month. Every stockbroker around is recommending investors buy it and the financial press is constantly raving about its management and business.

- The company is in an industry that everyone reckons is set to boom. However, by the time an industry is hot, the shares of companies in it are often too expensive.

- Directors are selling their shares.

- The share price has skyrocketed following a good news announcement.
- The share price keeps going up even when the company has bad news to announce.
- The sharemarket generally is flavour of the month. Everyone is talking about their share portfolio and exchanging 'can't lose' tips. These are classic signs of an overheated market. Be especially wary when people start arguing that 'The world has changed forever—the old rules of investing don't apply any more'. That's usually their way of explaining why they're paying far too much for their shares.

WHAT'S THE DIFFERENCE BETWEEN BUYING SHARES 'AT MARKET' AND 'AT LIMIT'?

At market means you buy or sell at the current market price. This means you are certain of making the transaction but you could end up with a price you are unhappy with if the market is extremely volatile or moving quickly.

At limit means you set a price limit on the transaction. But it pays to be flexible. If your limit is too low or high, the broker may not be able to make the trade and you could miss out on buying or selling.

YOU KEEP TALKING ABOUT DIVERSIFICATION—HOW MANY SHARES DO I NEED TO HOLD?

For true diversification across the different sectors of the market, you'd probably be looking at a portfolio of 20 companies or more. But that's a lot of companies to keep on top of. A better rule of thumb for less sophisticated investors, many brokers say, is to stick with five to 10 companies, each in a different sector of the market. And make up for the lack of real diversification by monitoring them closely and understanding what they do and what's likely to move their share price. Don't overlook managed funds as a way to supplement your share portfolio from a diversification point of view.

SMART TIP

Find out whether the companies you have invested in have a Dividend Reinvestment Plan. These plans let you receive new shares in the company instead of cash dividends. The new shares are issued directly by the company, which means you don't pay brokerage. Some companies also offer Dividend Reinvestment Plan shares on a discount on the market price. Reinvesting your dividends in this way allows you to benefit from compound interest.

HOW DO I KNOW WHEN TO SELL MY SHARES?

It's interesting that so much focus is placed on buying shares, and so little focus placed on the best time to sell them. But monitoring your share portfolio and making decisions on whether to keep your shares or get rid of them is an important part of the investment process. Here are a few of the triggers that might suggest it's time to sell:

- The outlook for the company has changed. Let's say you invested in Company X because it had a great business in a growth industry. But new management has come in and they're talking about selling that business to concentrate on something else. The reasons you invested in the company no longer apply.
- Your own circumstances have changed. Perhaps you started as a very aggressive investor but now find you can't afford to take big risks with your share portfolio. This could

indicate that it's time to sell some of those riskier shares and invest in something more conservative.

- The shares have become overpriced. I remember being told that 'You never go broke by taking a profit'. It was wise advice. Unfortunately, most investors are more inclined to hang on to their best-performing investments because they've fallen in love with them. They don't ask whether the shares are still a good investment proposition. Would you buy them at this price? If you can't bear the idea of selling out totally, an alternative is to take 'part profits'—brokerspeak for selling some of your shares and keeping the rest.

- You made a bad investment decision. Okay, it happens—even the best investors are known to pick bad investments from time to time. If you've done this, often the best course is to cut your losses and put what's left of your money some-where else. But don't make the mistake of selling a good investment just because it's going through a bad patch.

WHAT'S THE DIFFERENCE BETWEEN TRADING AND INVESTING? WON'T I MAKE MONEY FASTER BY TRADING?

Trading is trying to second guess what the market will do next; investing is selecting companies that will generate future profits. Traders tend to buy and sell their shares depending on what they think the market will do next, whereas investors tend to concentrate more on the longer term.

Many traders are what we call 'technical' traders, which means they use charts showing share price movements (and the volume of shares traded) to try to pick trends in where a share price is heading. Increased trading in a share, for example, may indicate that the market is becoming interested in it and it is about to take off. Some share traders will also 'short sell' shares. This means they borrow shares that they believe will fall in value from a broker for a fee, sell them, and then buy new cheaper shares later to repay their 'loan'. (The broker makes their money by charging a fee for the loan of the shares.)

When people think of getting rich quickly on the sharemarket, they're inevitably thinking of trading. But it's like the racetrack: you always hear about the small number of success stories, and you rarely hear about the much higher number of losses. The point is that there is no system that is 100 per cent failproof. The New Zealand Securities Commission has been concerned enough about some of the schemes being marketed to issue warnings to investors on blindly buying into systems that promise the world and don't deliver. If you want to trade, successful traders say it takes time and commitment. It's not something you can do when you have a spare hour on the weekend.

There are tax implications too: if you are trading (rather than investing) in shares your capital gains are taxable. The difference in your status as a trader or investor is deter-mined by your intention at the time of purchasing the shares. That can be rather difficult to prove. We recommend that if you are doing both you set up different portfolios (even going so far as to use a company structure for one portfolio) so that you avoid difficulties with the IRD.

MONEY ALERT

If you're still inclined towards trading, have a look at the research done by Professor Terrance Odean at the University of California's Graduate School of Management at www.gsm.ucdavis. He looked at the accounts of more than 35 000 households with a large discount brokerage firm between February 1991 and January 1997 and found that trading tended to be a wealth hazard rather than a wealth creator. The biggest problem, it appeared, was over-confidence—after a couple of successful trades, people traded more often and thought they could predict the markets. Online traders were the worst, and men did worse than women because they traded more often.

SHOULD I BORROW TO BUY SHARES? HOW DO I GO ABOUT IT?

Borrowing to buy shares has a couple of attractions. First, you can use other people's money to give yourself more investment firepower. Instead of investing, say, $1000, you can invest $5000. There are tax incentives too. You can normally claim the interest on your investment loan as a tax deduction, and you still get the benefits of any imputation credits on your dividends.

But there's one critical rule to remember if you're borrowing for any investment: Using borrowed money can increase your losses as well as your gains.

The main form of borrowing to buy shares is margin loans. You can use margin loans to buy shares or managed funds and you can generally borrow around 50 to 70 per cent of the value of the investment. So if you had $5000 to invest, you could borrow another $5000 to $10 000.

Most margin loans are interest only loans, which means you pay your interest each year, but you don't pay off any of the principal. At the end of the loan, you can either sell your investment to repay the loan or take out a new margin loan.

But there's one catch with these loans. If the value of your shares or funds falls by a pre-set limit—usually 5 or 10 per cent—you'll be hit with a 'margin call'. This means the lender will ask you to give them more cash or shares to restore the loan to the allowed ratio.

Let's say you took out a $10 500 margin loan to buy shares. You contributed $4500 of your own money, giving you a $15 000 investment with a borrowing ratio of 70 per cent. Your shares fall by 10 per cent, reducing the value of your investment to $13 500. Your loan is still $10 500 but that's now 78 per cent of the value of your investment. Your lender would want you to give it another $1050 to bring the borrowing ratio back to 70 per cent (that is, reduce your loan to $9450, making your total investment $13 950). If you couldn't find the cash, the lender would sell your shares to bring the loan back to the correct ratio.

For small investors, the minimum size of margin loans (often $20 000 or $50 000) can also be a problem. A personal loan is another option. A lot of investors also use home equity loans to invest in shares. These are loans that allow you to borrow against the increased equity you have in your home. For obvious reasons, these are more widely used by older people who are better established financially.

SMART TIP

 Many investors minimise the risk of margin calls by borrowing less than the allowable limit. This gives them a buffer against any falls in the value of their investment.

CHAPTER thirteen
Bricks and mortar—
investing in property

There used to be a saying that the seriously rich made their money in businesses and then maintained it by investing in property. That's not as true as it once was, but property still plays an important role in an investor's portfolio.

I'VE BEEN TOLD THAT NEGATIVE GEARING CAN SAVE ME PAYING SO MUCH TAX—SHOULD I BE DOING THAT?

There are so many get-rich-quick schemes that revolve around negative gearing that you'd think it was some sort of financial magic elixir. Not true. It's actually a very simple proposition. If you're borrowing to invest in an income-producing asset— such as a rental property—the tax office says you can claim a tax deduction on the costs of owning the investment. These costs include rates, repairs, insuring the property and any interest you pay on your investment loan. The trade-off is that you also have to pay tax on the income you receive—in this case, the rent from the property.

If your costs are higher than your income, you are negatively geared. What this means is that you're making a loss on your investment. Let's say you own a property that's earning $7500 a year in rent, but your costs are $10 000 a year. You have a net loss of $2500 and you can use this deduction to reduce your taxable income. That's why people talk about using negative gearing to get the tax man to help pay for their investment. If you're on the top marginal tax rate of 39 per cent, the example given means you'd save $975.00 in tax through negative gearing. If you were on the 33 per cent tax rate, your tax saving would be $825.00.

But if you looked closely at that example, you might have noticed two important things. The first is that the tax man only helps with part of your investment loss. You still have to find money out of your own pocket to make up the rest of the shortfall between your rent and your costs. Secondly, the tax savings are higher for people on high marginal tax rates— which makes negative gearing more attractive the more income you earn. So anyone who claims negative gearing is for everyone is spinning you a line.

Negative gearing tends to work best for high earners who have a secure income, can afford to fund the investment losses and see saving a bit in tax as a bonus. Lower earners may still find it advantageous to borrow to invest, but the emphasis should be more on the quality of the investment than on any tax magic—though that's probably good advice for everyone. Tax breaks alone are rarely a good reason for any decision.

SMART TIP

Negative gearing isn't just about property. You can also gear into managed funds or shares and get the same tax treatment. Indeed, as we discussed in Chapter 11, gearing into shares can work even better from a tax viewpoint, because you can also get tax breaks through the franking credits on your shares.

IS THERE ANY ADVANTAGE IN BUYING AN INVESTMENT PROPERTY NOW AND RENTING UNTIL I CAN BUY MY OWN HOME?

You'll need to do the numbers yourself to work out whether it's worthwhile—the answer depends very much on how much rent you have to pay, the size of your investment loan and the rent you get from the investment property. James, for example, bought an investment unit in Auckland's eastern suburbs, rented it out for a good price, and went into rented accommodation with a group of mates. The rent he was getting for the investment unit came very close to covering his mortgage payments and the rented accommodation was relatively good value. James figured he had a better lifestyle than he would have had struggling to pay a mortgage himself, and in the meantime he was building up an asset that he might sell to buy his own home later. He was also saving a small amount in tax, though this wasn't the objective.

CAN I RENT AN INVESTMENT PROPERTY TO MYSELF?

Not unless you want to make your life seriously complicated. People have come up with questionable schemes where they buy the property in the name of a company or trust and rent it out to themselves, but it's complicated, and you're playing with fire with the IRD.

I'D LIKE TO BUY A NEW HOME BUT KEEP MY EXISTING HOME AS AN INVESTMENT. CAN I BORROW AGAINST THE VALUE OF MY OLD PLACE (AS AN INVESTMENT PROPERTY) TO BUY A NEW ONE TO LIVE IN AND CLAIM A TAX DEDUCTION ON THE INTEREST?

You're getting into muddy waters. When the IRD decides whether or not you should get tax breaks on your loan, it looks at the purpose of the borrowings, not what property you are using as security for the loan. In this case, it would be easy for the tax office to say the purpose of your borrowings is to buy a new house for yourself—nothing to do with investing.

SMART TIP

Talk to a good accountant about the best way to structure your borrowings so you don't fall foul of the tax man. It's well worth the cost!

HOW DO I CHOOSE AN INVESTMENT PROPERTY?

Lots of people start off with an investment property near where they live. They know the area and they know the market. But while a good investment property will have many of the same features as a good home investment, you need to focus on how attractive your investment property is to both tenants and future buyers. Here are some of the things to look for:

Where it is

If you can afford a waterfront property, go for it. Even water glimpses are popular. Away from the water, people prefer to look out at attractive parkland, gardens or city vistas than at the brick wall of the building next door. Lots of people prefer a property on the high side of the street. They're less likely to flood and have better 'presence'. You also want an investment that's close to amenities—parks, schools, hospitals, shops and public transport. If you want to rent your property, ask yourself, too, whether the area is attractive to cashed-up tenants. How far do you have to walk for a good cappuccino? What about things like smart restaurants and delis?

Who wants to live there

Talk to the local real estate agents and flick through the 'to let' ads in the local paper. You want to invest in an area that's popular with renters but not one where there are too many places available. (You can tell if there are too many rental properties about if the same ads keep popping up every week—especially if the advertised rents keep getting cheaper.) Look for a property with something special that will help attract tenants.

What it earns and costs

How much can you reasonably rent the property for? Often the agent selling the property will give you an estimate of what they think it could rent for. But remember, this agent is acting for the vendor of the property, not you. If the figure seems high, check with other agents. If the property is already rented, get confirmation of the rent and find out how long the tenant has been in the property, and how long it was vacant before being rented at that price. It doesn't happen often, but you do get sharp vendors who will 'rent' their property to a mate at an inflated price to make the property a better proposition for investors. When you buy, you may find the mate moves out and you can't rent it at anything like the artificial rent you were quoted. This has also happened with some developers, who offered properties with 'guaranteed' rents for the first six or 12 months.

When you're looking at financial viability, you'll also need to take into account other costs: rates, insurance, body corporate costs or levies (if you're buying a unit), agent's fees and repairs and maintenance.

SMART TIP

If you want to sound as if you know your stuff, work out the yield on potential investment properties. It's easy. Simply work out what you can earn in annual rent, allowing for a period of around four weeks when the property is untenanted. Then work out your likely annual costs. What's left over when you deduct these costs from the rent? If you divide what's left over into the cost of the property and turn the result into a percentage, you'll get the 'yield' on your investment.

Let's say you're thinking of buying a unit for $150 000. You can rent it for $200 week, giving you an annual rent of $9600 after allowing for vacancies. Divide that into $150 000; multiply by 100; and you have the gross yield on the investment—6.4 per cent. You'll find real estate agents will quote gross yields on investment properties because they sound better. But from your point of view, it's the money in your hand that counts, not just the rent. If the annual expenses on this unit were $3000, you'd have a net rent of $6600. Your net yield would be 4.4 per cent.

Knowing the likely yield on investments allows you to compare the rental returns from different properties and can help you judge their value.

What sort of shape it's in

As a property investor, you'll want a low-maintenance property. The last thing you want is to be constantly doing expensive repairs. Get a building inspection before you buy. This can uncover any lurking nasties and give you an idea of what you might be up for in repair costs. If you're buying a unit, also make sure you check the building's records—these will generally include things like any special levies that are planned to pay for repairs and any known problems that have already been identified.

I'VE BEEN TO A SEMINAR WHERE THEY WERE SAYING YOU COULD MAKE BIG MONEY BUYING OFF THE PLAN—IS THIS TRUE?

When you buy off the plan, you pay a small deposit now and the rest of the money when the building is completed. If demand is strong, you may find you can re-sell your property at a profit before completion, without having to find the bulk of the money for your purchase. Developers also arrange deposit bonds, where instead of paying the deposit, you pay an even smaller fee to the deposit bond company which guarantees the deposit will be paid by you. So if you can sell at a profit before completion, you've made a large amount of money on a small investment.

The people who run these seminars tend to make this sound like a foolproof plan. But it's not. Your property may not have risen in value before the building was completed. Indeed there are often 'distress' sales at this time as buyers who can't afford to pay for their units put them on the market. There may be faults in the building that need fixing before re-selling is a viable proposition. In addition, other competing developments may have come onto the market offering better deals to buyers.

This isn't to say you can't do well by buying off the plan. Developers will often offer discounts to get buyers locked in early. But you need to investigate carefully things like the size of the property, the quality of the finishes and fittings, and the reputation of the builder. It's also a good idea to check to see whether other competing developments will be coming onto the market.

I'VE SEEN A GREAT PLACE TO BUY AS A HOLIDAY HOME—CAN I STILL CLAIM ALL THE TAX DEDUCTIONS THAT YOU GET FOR INVESTMENT PROPERTIES?

The tax man has been cracking down on rental properties in recent years, and holiday homes are right in his sights. There's no problem with buying an investment property in a holiday area, letting it out and claiming the costs as a tax deduction. If you want to do this with your mates, the income from the property and the expenses can simply be split between you in proportion to your share in the property. But what gets up the tax man's nose is people who buy a holiday property, claim all the tax deductions and then live in it themselves. You can only claim tax deductions for the periods when it was available for rent to the general public—not when you or your friends were staying there.

DO I NEED A REAL ESTATE AGENT TO RENT MY PROPERTY OR CAN I DO IT MYSELF?

It depends on the time and effort you're prepared to put into it. Agents' fees have been deregulated and can vary, but generally you'll pay around 5 to 8 per cent of rent for an agent to manage your property for you. In return for that, they should find tenants for your property, organise the lease, collect the rent, arrange for necessary repairs and monitor your property for you. You're also likely to be asked to pay a 'letting fee' of one week's rent when the agency finds you a tenant, and some out-of-pocket expenses, such as the costs for advertising for new tenants and repair work.

Whether you do this work yourself or opt for an agent, there are a few things you should insist on. You, or the agent, should check tenants' references before you agree to rent them the property. It's much easier to keep bad tenants out than to try to get rid of them once they've moved in. You, or the agent, must also be vigilant with making sure the rent is paid on time. It's much harder to get back rent once it starts to mount up. The person managing the property needs to keep up to date with what other properties are renting for to ensure that your property is getting the right price. And they should conduct six-monthly or annual inspections of the property—both to ensure that the tenant is looking after it and to identify any maintenance work that's needed to keep it in good shape.

If you decide to go with an agent, look for one who will commit to doing all these things. Ask other investors for recommendations—they'll be only too pleased to tell you who is worth the money and who isn't.

HOW DO I FINANCE AN INVESTMENT PROPERTY?

Most borrowers simply use an ordinary home loan that is secured by the investment property. The days when you had to take out a more expensive investment loan are gone—and good riddance too. Some investors prefer to use fixed rate loans to buy investment properties because this makes budgeting easier. Some lenders may even allow you to take out an 'interest only' loan where you pay the interest each year but don't repay the principal until the end of the loan—when you will presumably sell the property for a profit. The good thing about an interest only loan is that you can use all your excess savings to reduce your non-tax-deductible home loan instead of paying off the principal on your investment loan. You pay your home off faster and maximise your tax deductions. The danger is that the loan may expire at a bad time to sell, in which case you'll need to refinance your loan.

Other options include things like home equity loans, but these are better for older people who are using the equity they've built up in their own homes as a basis for investing. If you're thinking of investing in something outside the traditional rental unit—such as a shop or business premises—it may be worth using a mortgage broker who can find the best loan for you.

CHAPTER fourteen
The inevitables—
death and taxes

It's a bit of a downer to have to think about these subjects, isn't it? But taxes are compulsory and death is no optional extra either. So what do they both mean financially?

DO I HAVE TO DO A TAX RETURN?

The taxation system in New Zealand is so straightforward for people on PAYE (Pay as You Earn) that most people do not have to file a tax return as long as their only income is through a wage or salary. The tax of wage and salary earners is paid through employers and is usually correct to the last cent—if you have given your employer the correct tax code for your circumstances.

If you are self-employed or receive income from a business or from overseas or receive income that was not taxed at source you will need to fill in an IR3 tax form.

If you are uncertain about your status you should call the IRD. They can also provide a Personal Tax Summary (PTS) that is a record of your earnings and the tax you have paid. This will allow you to check the information and you might be able to claim expenses or rebates. You may be paying child support, for example, but are being taxed under the wrong code.

HOW MUCH TAX DO I HAVE TO PAY?

New Zealand's tax system is relatively simple and straight-forward for wage and salary earners. It is a progressive scale—you pay more tax on income above certain levels.

The rate at present for income under $38 000 is 19.5 per cent. On income between $38 000 and $60 000 you pay 33 per cent and on income over $60 000 you pay 39 per cent.

There are low-earner rebates for people who earn below $38 000, for those still at school, or younger than 15 years old, etc., but you do have to fill in an IR526 form to claim them.

I'VE ALWAYS PREPARED MY OWN TAX RETURN—WHAT ARE THE ADVANTAGES OF GETTING AN ACCOUNTANT TO PREPARE IT FOR ME?

Most wage and salary earners in New Zealand don't have to fill in a tax return at all. If you have additional income from other sources, are self-employed or are in business you will have to file a tax return. If your affairs are at all complicated you would be best advised to consult an accountant.

Accountants are used for more complicated tax returns and can also advise on other issues, such as the best way to structure your investments or to borrow money for investing. They will generally charge for their services on an hourly basis. You can keep these costs under control by doing a bit of homework before you go to see your accountant. If you've sorted through all your records, they'll have less work to do than if you turn up with a shoebox full of bits of paper.

Look for an accountant who is a member of an industry body such as the Institute of Chartered Accountants. Ask others for a recommendation—you will want someone who is competent but also easy to deal with and who can give you good advice. Having a helpful accountant will be a great benefit as you grow your investments and wealth and as your financial affairs become more complicated.

SMART TIP

Be very wary of any accountant who tells you that you don't have to worry about records or that you can claim deductions that seem dodgy. *You* are the person who has to sign the tax return, and if you're audited and your claims are found to be false, you're the one who will have to pay the penalties. The fact that your accountant told you what to do is irrelevant.

WHAT SORTS OF EXPENSES CAN I CLAIM?

Wage and salary earners can claim virtually none.

If you are self-employed or own a business, the basic rule is that you can only claim on money spent in connection with earning your income. This means that you may be able to claim a portion of your home costs because you run your business from there. This could include a proportion of your heating, maintenance and even rental costs. Most of your direct business expenses such as telephone, postage and motor vehicle maintenance would be deductible. However, tax is always complicated and you do not want to get it wrong. For example, although you may be able to claim a lot of your vehicle expenses you will also be liable for Fringe Benefit Tax (FBT) for the personal use of the vehicle!

The IRD provides useful booklets for people in these positions or you can check their Website (www.ird.govt.nz). It may be more efficient to use an accountant who is accustomed to dealing with small businesses. If your affairs are very complicated—you have several types of investment, are involved in a number of businesses, have one or more trust, etc.—you will probably want to deal with a specialist tax accountant. Tax is very complicated when you go beyond simple wage and salary earners and you can save yourself a lot of money through good advice. Remember, too, that you are ultimately responsible for the information on your tax return—if the IRD decides that the tax return that is filed is incorrect they will pursue you for the extra tax payable and you may incur heavy penalties. It is not worth getting your taxation wrong. As they say, good advice is expensive but poor advice is even more expensive!

In order to be able to claim expenses associated with investments, many investors form a company through which they run their property or share portfolios. Again, you will need to get the advice of a good accountant to form the right structure to suit your needs.

HOW LIKELY AM I TO BE FOUND OUT IF I FIB IN MY TAX RETURN?

Our tax system operates on the basis of self-assessment. This means that the IRD accepts the figures that you lodge each year without checking them. But it has various programs in place to catch tax cheats and the penalties are tough if you're found to have fibbed. While the IRD can, and does, do random audits, it also has ways of targeting people who are more likely to have problems with their tax returns.

For instance, it has computer systems that can track the interest paid on bank accounts, dividends on shares, and so on, and check these against your tax return. It's easy to overlook declaring a few dollars in interest when you fill in your tax return, but if you do you may get a 'please explain' letter from the IRD.

Accountants say you're also likely to draw attention if your refund suddenly increases by a large amount, or your claims exceed the average for your industry. And in recent years the IRD has been targeting areas where it believes there is a higher incidence of tax being underpaid. Recent areas targeted include deductions on rental properties, and people not declaring dividends. Do you really want to take the chance?

WHAT SORTS OF RECORDS DO I NEED TO KEEP FOR MY TAXES?

Most people won't need to keep much as there is little they can claim. You should of course keep your bank records (and also check that the bank has your IRD number and is deducting the right amount of tax from any interest you are earning).

You can claim on charitable donations you make to a maximum of $1500 donated but you will need receipts to prove the donations were made.

Obviously, if you are claiming tax rebates on imputed dividends you will need copies of dividend statements and other documentation received.

If you have rental properties and want to claim for expenses incurred in your investment you will need to keep receipts for work done, good records of your costs, etc.

Business owners will probably have considerable expenses to claim and should set up and maintain good record systems—not only will this make it easier for you to claim expenses, but a good system will reduce your accounting fees and reduce the likelihood of any difficulties with the IRD.

Things for which you do not get a written receipt, for example, parking money, should be recorded in a notebook/diary. While many of these expenses are individually small, they mount up to a great deal of money over a year. And it's your money!

HOW LONG DO I NEED TO KEEP MY RECORDS?

You generally need to keep them for seven years from the date you lodge your tax return. If you have a dispute with the tax office, you need to keep them until the dispute is resolved. If you're writing off or 'depreciating' the cost of something over time (common examples are computers and some rental property expenses) you'll need to keep the records for seven years after the last claim was made.

WHEN SHOULD I DRAW UP A WILL?

Lots of people say that everyone over 18 should have a will. But the best test is to ask what you want to happen to your assets if you die. If you have clear ideas on who should get what, you definitely need a will. If you die 'intestate' (without a will), your assets will be distributed to your next of kin according to a legal formula. For some people, this is okay. But the formula is unlikely to include people you may want to leave some of your possessions to—such as your girlfriend or best mate.

There are cheap do-it-yourself will kits on the market that are okay for very simple wills, though you might still want to get a lawyer to cast an eye over the finished product. Or you can pay a lawyer to draft a will for you. The main requirements are that the will be signed at the end (on the bottom of each page is even better), then dated and signed by two witnesses who can verify that you signed it.

MONEY ALERT

If you die intestate and have no living relatives, your money can go to the government. So draw up a will to avoid this happening.

WHAT DO I PUT IN MY WILL?

There are no hard and fast rules. Wills can be extremely complex and legalistic or simple, handwritten notes.

Start with a list of all your assets. Then work out who you want to leave them to. Like it or not, the law requires you to make provision for family members and dependants, so if you want to leave someone out, get legal advice first. Think carefully about how you word your will—there are times when you can be too specific. If you want to leave your car to your boyfriend, for example, refer in your will to 'my car' not 'my Hyundai'. That way your wishes will still be carried out even if you sell your Hyundai and buy a Mazda. Also make sure you include a 'residual' clause to cover the stuff that you haven't itemised in the will.

You'll also need to nominate an executor for your will. This is the person who will administer the will to make sure your wishes are carried out. Most people use family members or friends as their executors, but make sure you ask them first! Your executor should also be given a copy of your will (you can put it in a sealed envelope if you don't want them to know what it says) and told where the original is kept. Lawyers and trustee companies can also be appointed as executors to your will—they will charge a fee for this to your estate.

Keep your will in a safe place and don't forget to update it if your circumstances or wishes change.

WHAT HAPPENS TO MY DEBTS IF I DIE?

Your debts don't die with you, unfortunately. Your creditors can pursue your estate for their money. So if you're leaving your car to your cousin, remember that you're leaving them your debt as well.

DO I NEED LIFE INSURANCE?

Let's be honest here: life insurance is of no benefit at all to you. It's there to provide for the people you care about if something happens to you. So it's much more important for people with dependants than for singles who are footloose and fancy free.

If you think you need life insurance—maybe you've just taken out a mortgage and don't want your partner saddled with all your debts if you're not around—the objective is to cover yourself for enough to ensure your loved ones are able to survive financially when you're gone. You might want to insure your life for the amount of your outstanding debts. Or maybe for a couple of years' income? If you're a homemaker, the question to ask is how much it would cost to hire someone to fill your shoes.

The good news is that life insurance is relatively cheap for younger people. You can get a couple of hundred thousand dollars' worth of cover for a few hundred dollars a year. Life insurance is cheaper if you don't smoke, and it's cheaper for women because they live longer.

But even if you don't need life insurance, think about whether you need another form of personal insurance— income protection insurance. Your ability to earn an income for the next 30 or 40 years is without doubt your most valuable asset. If you're earning $30 000 a year, you have the potential to earn $1.2 million over the next 40 years. But if you get sick or disabled, and are unable to work, that's money you won't get.

Income protection insurance, or disability insurance, as it's also known, pays you up to 75 per cent of your income if you are unable to work because of illness or disability (but not because you have lost your job). Women tend to pay more for disability insurance than men (they're more likely to be disabled), and the premiums vary according to your occupation. As a rule of thumb, white-collar workers will generally pay less for disability insurance than manual workers.

Other forms of life insurance you may consider are trauma insurance, which pays you a lump sum if you are diagnosed with certain life-threatening conditions, and total and permanent disability insurance, which pays you a lump sum if you're seriously disabled.

Index